BIG LITTLE BOOK OF
PLAYBOY
Limericks

BIG LITTLE BOOK OF
PLAYBOY
Limericks

EDITORS OF **PLAYBOY**

Illustrations by LeRoy Neiman

Main Street
A division of Sterling Publishing Co., Inc.
New York

A Main Street Book

©2005 **PLAYBOY**
Published 2005 by Main Street, a division of Sterling Publishing Co., Inc.

Distributed in Canada by Sterling Publishing
c/o Canadian Manda Group, 165 Dufferin Street
Toronto, Ontario M6K 3H6

Distributed in Great Britain by Chrysalis Books
64 Brewery Road, London N79NT, England

Distributed in Australia by Capricorn Link (Australia) Pty. Ltd.
P.O. Box 704, Windsor, NSW 2756, Australia

Playboy and Rabbit Head design are trademarks of Playboy Enterprises International, Inc.

ISBN 1-4027-3013-6

Femlin illustrations by LeRoy Neiman
Designed by Jeffrey Rutzky

Printed in the United States of America

10 9 8 7 6 5 4 3 2 1

Contents

Preface: Anatomy of a Limerick

Serious limericists are a particular bunch. They take their craft very seriously, and it's not at all hard to see why: the limerick, though undeniably a form of poetic verse, is nonetheless the black sheep of the family. In order to foster wider acceptance of the form, dedicated archivists and composers of limericks work hard to set, and to some extent enforce, rules and regulations. To these valiant champions, apologies are offered in advance; for while the technical definition of the limerick will dutifully be laid out here, it is our general contention that rigid adherence to the "classic" recipe undermines the sense of fun that is the hallmark of a good limerick. In fact, rule-breaking itself—in form, content, and even taste— is, to our minds, also an essential ingredient. Given our position, it should come as no surprise that the limericks in this book range from the classic to the *outré* (in absolutely every sense of the word).

Of course, you can't have rule-breaking without rules, so let's take a look at them.

The classic limerick is a poem of five lines, the first, second, and fifth of which end with the same rhyme; the third and fourth lines, which are shorter than the others, rhyme with each other.

Rhythmically speaking, the first, second, and fifth lines have three metric feet, one iamb and two anapests, trailed by an unaccented syllable; the third and fourth lines have two metric feet, one iamb and one anapest. An iamb has two syllables, the second of which is accented (i-AMB) and the anapest has three, the third of which is accented (a-na-PEST). To illustrate, here is the classic limerick form, rendered syllabically:

i-AMB a-na-PEST a-na-PEST a
i-AMB a-na-PEST a-na-PEST a
i-AMB a-na-PEST
i-AMB a-na-PEST
i-AMB a-na-PEST a-na-PEST a

But perhaps most notably, the limerick is a narrative marvel. The best examples tell an entire story—complete with twist of fate, savage comeuppance, regrettable exposure, or comical misstep—in five short lines. Formally speaking, the fifth line is the cornerstone of the whole structure, the place where the story is brought to a close and where the whammy is delivered.

So much for the rules, which are simple enough—now for the *je ne sais quoi* at the heart of the matter. The spirit of the limerick, from Edward Lear's day to now, has always been a mischievous one. And in the modern period, these little ditties have taken on a decidedly adult tone, focusing as they tend to do on details involving the most intimate physical and emotional terrain. It would be a mistake to think that this mischievousness is limited to the content, however; it also manifests itself in the liberties that are frequently taken with structure, rhyme, and meter. And given the importance of that fifth line, it is no accident that much of the tomfoolery happens right there. So, purists be warned: many of the limericks in this book have too many or too few syllables per line, lines that don't rhyme where they should, too many lines (or not quite enough), and frequently deal with the most sensitive subject matter imaginable. Enjoy!

—Benjamin Mott,
New York

Introduction

If you say to a literate guy, "Limericks!," comes a gleam in his eye and he quotes one or two; if he can't tell a few, then, beware; he's an enemy spy.

—**Anonymous, composer of limericks**

As one literary genre after another has, in our media-drenched civilization, gone sterile, the limerick has retained its pristine, antiquated elegance and its caustic wit, as this generous collection of limericks (many of which are taken from the jokes page of *Playboy*) happily demonstrates.

A host of traditional, familiar limericks is included here. These are the precious heirlooms of our talented ancestors who, often by oral tradition and in defiance of recurring periods of censorship, have bequeathed them to posterity, just as the ancient troubadours passed their poetry on to subsequent generations.

The best limericks have an aura of timelessness about them, and have for generations inspired delight in readers and listeners receptive to the form's off-color charms. Limericks should be told with due reverence to all, whether old or young—for nobody is safe from skewering. And, come to think of it, the younger the audience, the better (to a point, of course, for the content of the classic limerick is undeniably blue): unfortunately, this truly magnificent form of literary expression is blatantly ignored in college curricula, even at the graduate level, despite the fact that it is headier than weed, punchier than liquor, more sensuous than secret vice, and only slightly inferior to the act of love itself (not to mention fertile training ground for outrageous exaggeration).

Scattered throughout this book are scores of limericks that have rarely, if ever, before been published between the covers of a book. Some of these have been composed by old hands, some by relative newcomers. Incidentally, a word of warning: So beguiling is the art of creating limericks that once it has been ventured, today's beginner speedily becomes tomorrow's expert. Let the fiendish practice get its grip, and then just try and stop after composing only one limerick. Go ahead—I dare you.

Indeed, it is the aspiration of every limerick-lover to compose, during a lifetime of indolence and folly, at least one perfect limerick that will survive him and become a classic, a part of the immortal canon. Several

LeRoy Neiman

of the limericks in this collection bid fair to receive such an accolade, to the glory of the composers who, like so many authors of yore, must paradoxically remain anonymous. All hail to the success of their efforts!

A first-rate limerick features the humorous touch of a P.J. O'Rourke, the mordant wit of an Oscar Wilde, and the shock value of an X-rated film. So potent is the limerick's power, in fact, that many hosts and hostesses forbid their recital, for once the guests start telling limericks, it is goodbye to gossip, ecology, politics, and even to furtive dalliance in the kitchen or greenhouse—limericks truly are that enthralling, *especially* in mixed company.

The basic requirement for great limericks is that they be humorous. "But what is *humor*?" one may rightly ask. Many serious attempts have been made to explain it and to define it by categories or cases. One intriguing theory claims that all humor can be boiled down to three situations: witnessing another being cuckolded, or criticized in the midst of his lovemaking; witnessing another being robbed or caught up in his own machinations; or witnessing another taking a pratfall or suffering an equally deflating experience. In each of these cases lies the basic mechanics of humor: the opportunity to laugh at what happens to *another*. Freud himself demonstrated how pleasant his subjects found it to witness unfortunate events happening to other people—events that the observers would certainly not wish to happen to themselves.

The cornerstone of a great limerick is its fifth line, which can fairly be called the banana peel of poetry. The first four lines serve to prepare the audience for the coming humiliation or pratfall, and then the glorious fifth line delivers the whammy. To wit: For an amorous swain, confident and cocky at his work, to be interrupted in his ardor by the woman's remark in the fifth line, "You've got it all in but the head" or "This won't be much of a sin" or "You mean it ain't your finger?" reveals there is always a banana peel lurking for the unwary.

The origin of the word *limerick* is unknown, although there have been many theories regarding its etymology. It is generally acknowledged that the name does not have anything to do with County Limerick in Ireland or the town of Limerick or with the Earl of Limerick and his charming duchess (who is just a dear friend, by the way, no more). Traces of the form have been found in early literature, in folk ballads, in Shakespeare, and so on. Whatever its first origins may have been and what influence they have had on the modern limerick's form,* it is commonly accepted that these little verses began to be called limericks around the middle of the nineteenth century.

In 1846, Edward Lear, the godfather of the limerick, published his *A Book of Nonsense*. In all, Lear composed more than two hundred limericks. For him, the limerick was in the tradition of his light verse, gossamer and airy (and clean) bits of whimsy, faultlessly versified. Lear often coined his own words for the purposes of versification, and the puckish quality of "The Owl and the Pussycat" is everywhere in evidence. However, in almost all of Lear's limericks, the rhyme (last) word of the first line is repeated as the last word of the fifth line. But many have overlooked the fact that Lear on occasion did use three *different* rhyme words, as in the following:

There was a Young Lady whose eyes
Were unique as to color and size;
    When she opened them wide,
    People all turned aside,
And started away in surprise.

*For a historical and scholarly description of the origins and growth of the limerick, as well as a very solid bibliography, see William S. Baring-Gould's brilliant introduction to his *The Lure of the Limerick* (New York: Clarkson N. Potter, 1967).

Admittedly, Lear's last line is not very humorous. But the use of three different rhyme words contains the germ of what was to come. It remained, near the turn of the century, for the fifth line to evolve into the coruscating gem it is today; at about the same time, the limerick turned obscene. And then how its popularity grew!

Early dissemination of the limerick, in no small measure due to the increasing obscenity, was largely oral, as it so often still is today. Consequently, many of the older limericks have numerous variants. The man who "put it in double" may come from Ghent or from Kent. Variants are especially common in the fifth line. The young man from Racine, who invented that remarkable machine (for which, it seems, he never got a patent), has a number of fifth lines, to wit:

> ...Entertaining itself in between.
> ...And guaranteed used by the queen.
> ...With a drip-pot to catch all the cream.
> ...And jerked itself off in between.
> ...The God-damndest thing ever seen.
> ...With attachments for those in between.
> And so on and so forth....

Who is to say which of these is the best? And anyway, why spoil the delight of the experts who, after the limerick has been told in one version, then proceed to recite, at carefully timed intervals, alternate fifth lines, to the increasing hilarity of the audience? Frequently, as every reciter of limericks knows, it is the cumulative effect of several ribald ditties, delivered one hard upon the other, that gets the most enthusiastic response from the audience.

There have been many attempts, and not always commendable ones, to improve upon the classics. This is another cause of variant versions. The Racine limerick is among the most widely known and recited ones, so it is not surprising that it has such a wealth of fifth lines. One should not be too hard on those who tinker with the classics. Have you never felt the urge to add some ad hoc obscenity to a current pop song or classic rock chestnut?

Variants also may arise because the reciter forgets the exact rhyme word and coins an equivalent (*Kent* for *Ghent*, for example). It is even easier to forget the exact words of lines three and four, and an impromptu version is thereby frequently created out of necessity—and sometimes it is superior to the original. But one man's favorite may not be another's. Do not interrupt the laughter at the end of a limerick with a pedantic, "No, no! It goes like this…." It is far better, as the laughter dies down, to add your version as an afterthought. Play your cards in this spirit of cooperation and you may get the bigger laugh and even reap the pleasure of seeing the original teller of the limerick furtively jot down your line.

The purpose of the limerick, as already mentioned, is to amuse and entertain. Some of the classics have been deliberately excluded from this collection, mainly because they are witless and in poor taste, despite their considerable popularity. They more often receive a supercilious snicker than a hearty guffaw. In these cases, we have deemed the banana peel to have lost some of its slickness. Such limericks may help explain why some people claim to detest limericks and, at the first iambic indication of one, take off for the loo, presumably there to relieve themselves (mainly of your artistic expression, of course).

In the attempt to find challenging and novel rhyme words, astute limerick researchers have used most of the countries and cities of the world. It would require a geographical expert to locate every such place correctly on the map. Newcomers to the field are sometimes surprised to discover that the most popular limerick country is Peru. What is the fatal attraction of this innocent little country? The answer lies in the number of common words that rhyme with it: *canoe, do, coo, woo, Jew, pew, new, knew, threw, through, blew, blue, spew, stew, gnu, flu, flew, sou, few, cockatoo, zoo, true, glue, two, to;* all these have been used, as has *screw you, too!* For similar reasons, limericks about Bombay, France, Khartoum, Madras, Madrid (and Spain as a whole), and Siam abound.

If the limerick has nearly exhausted the countries and cities of the world, what about the *dramatis personae* of the limerick? As might be expected, there is almost no profession that has not been honored, almost no job, be it ever so humble, that has not been touched upon. The army, navy, air force, and marines; the medical profession (doctors, dentists, surgeons, morticians, obstetricians, even Dr. Freud); musicians ranging from the aloof maestro to a simple flautist, plus a goodly company of famous composers; artists, painters, writers; world-famous figures from Gandhi and Napoleon to De Gaulle. From less exalted ranks come athletes and bums, cowboys and gauchos, bakers and barbers, plumbers, tailors, jewelers, gardeners, teachers and students, seamstresses, male chauvinists, feminists, a cabby's wife, even a Hindu mahout. Oddly, the one profession seldom glorified in the limerick is the legal one (as opposed its popularity as a subject in your garden-variety one-liner or shaggy dog).

Far and away the most popular target for limericks is the clergy. There are hundreds upon hundreds of limericks that deal with the men and women of the church, many of which are included in this volume. Very few are complimentary. According to the majority of limericks, the practitioners of organized religion are men and women of considerable appetites (but then again, sin is in the eye of the beholder, is it not?).

The majority of clerical limericks are concerned with the lowly: the curate, the monk, the parson, the preacher, and the vicar appear with some frequency, and the misunderstood priest more than that. The overall picture of the religious professional they foster is a pretty shabby and scandalous one. Only on rare occasions does a limerick treat the man or woman of God gently or even with grudging respect. Most of the participants are meek about their sins and accept their condemnation humbly, but this monotony is relieved by an occasional rakish and defiant servant of the Church with a true flair for disreputable behavior.

The curate is criticized, mostly by women, for his lack of ardor. The monk is often pictured as licentious, as are the nuns. The parson is an object of scorn; the preacher suffers from constipation and flatulation and preaches at such length his faithful flock threatens to stuff him with firecrackers. The vicar gets more sympathetic treatment, although he is occasionally warned of strangulation if he insists upon singing at services.

The poor priest is the common butt for all dissatisfaction with religious practices. He is the link between the people and the Church. Again and again he is pictured as committing various acts of depravity, being immoral in the confessional, afflicted with venereal disease, and, on top of all that, stingy and critical to excess.

So much for the lower ranks. Limericks mention all those high in the clerical establishment, too, but these exemplars are generally treated with some measure of respect. The pope, the cardinal, and the archbishop are all mentioned (although this latter worthy, as we will see, is cited for acts of fornication). But the main culprit among the higher orders is the bishop. Here we are now far enough down the hierarchical line to find the scapegoat for the establishment, as the priest was for the lesser clergy. There exist dozens of limericks devoted to bishops in which these worthies get their comeuppance. He commits frequent intercourse (and, unlike others, is very adept at it, managing thirteen with the wife of the dean, for instance), practices incest, and even keeps young owls for immoral purposes. As a price for his sins, he is sometimes known to suffer from elephantiasis.

So much for the clergy. Where there is smoke there is often a friar. But it must be pointed out that most of the accusations against the clergy could probably have been made against Napoleon, Henry James, or Toulouse-Lautrec. And about many other people we know!

The limerick encompasses the whole universe in microcosm. Future sociologists and psychologists will study it as a fascinating aspect of social psychology. It is a veritable *Who's Who* of social, artistic, and political fame. It immortalizes scandalous gossip. The name of Magda Lupescu, for example, is on more tongues than that of the king she was under. And the limerick about Elizabeth Barrett might just possibly be better known than most of her poetry. Rose madder is as well known as Titian, and that famous statue of Phidias is familiar to thousands who have never seen it. And Gloria has made the long-defunct house band at the Waldorf Astoria forever immortal.

Many people aspire to compose limericks of their own, despite the fact that the art is more devilishly difficult than it looks. It is not easy to compose a limerick, and even great poets had their difficulties. Those who do not possess a well-developed sense of rhythm and meter should devote their energies to declaiming limericks, letting them flow forth like veritable geysers of wit for an enchanted throng. But if one has the rhyming ability and a modicum of waggery, have at it (and with our blessings)!

Here are some general bits of advice that may be helpful to the determined beginner. In the first place, try starting with the fifth line. This line is the crux of a good limerick. If you do not have a great one at the start, you are likely to waste your talents on four good lines, only to find that the limerick goes down the drain for lack of the fifth line, like a drama with two good acts and a wretched third. The fifth line may be almost anything: the punch line of a story, or an outrageous pun, or a switch on some current slogan or famous name, or just some little line of your own that scans perfectly and scintillates with wit. As a test of creative ability and genius, we encourage the aspirant poet to try rewriting the fifth lines of the limericks in this collection.

The first and second lines usually work in tandem to set the scene, geographically and physically. They should build up an aura of suspense, impending excitement, or doom (don't neglect to throw down that banana peel!). It is sometimes necessary to invent a proper name or a place to provide a sufficient number of rhyme words. If someone challenges your geography, just say it is a town in Uttar Pradesh or a village due north of Ulan Bator. The classic structure of "There was a young lady [or fellow] from…" has given way to various opening lines, such as "Said a civil rights worker named Dot," or "A worried young man from Stamboul."

The third and fourth lines are generally used to further the plot, whetting the appetite for the denouement. These two lines often determine the final elegance of the limerick. They should be a pyrotechnical display of the composer's power of language and poetical instinct. How charming to find lines like "While in her interstices/Lurked a far worse disease" and "The weather's too sultry/To commit adult'ry." *Summa cum laude!*

Frequently, limericks must be worked over and over. Often they must be put aside to await a blessing from the Muse, and sometimes even thrown away entirely in favor of a new start. Nothing does more harm to a limerick than a line that limps. It can never be excused. But if the main idea for the limerick is sparkling, witty, and novel and the rhymes good, it will eventually work out and the thrill of the completed gem is one of life's signal pleasures. As a toiler in the vineyard once wrote:

> Yᴏᴜ labor from midnight to morn,
> Consuming a gallon of corn.
>   The last line comes neatly,
>   You pass out completely,
> And thus is a limerick born.

Endless variations of the standard five-line limerick have been perpetrated: two-liners, three-liners, six-liners; limericks with extra long fifth lines and extra short ones; with rhymes such as St. Bees, wasp, and hornet; with surprise endings; with endless repetition, such as the young lady from Spain (or from Maine) who did it "again and again and again and again." There is a limerick composed entirely of the syllable "da" scanning perfectly for four lines and all of the fifth fine except the last syllable, which is any four-letter word desired. There is a limerick beginning "There was a young man from Racine/Birmingham, Wheeling, Moline," continuing to the end with places made famous by limericks. There are also a few limericks in Latin, French, German, Spanish, Russian, and even Swahili. As far as we're concerned, though, all of them prove conclusively that English is the mother tongue of the limerick.

These little tricks aside, there has been little change in the limerick form since the nineteenth century. This may very well be for the best, but one variation of note has appeared in that time. It consists of a number of third and fourth lines within the classical body of the limerick. There may be two sets or several. It permits detailed background, intense character development and delineation, and the evolution of a complicated story, while at the same time taxing the composer's poetic talents. Since these added sequences are all in the middle of the limerick, they are referred to as "the inner limerick." The following is one of the longest, and even if it does not become popular it may triple the number of people traveling by air:

A voluptuous maiden named Wright
Took a 747 one night.
  The salesman beside her
  Was first to bestride her.
  He found her too ample,
  But left a small sample,
  Though he nearly was trapped
  When his seat belt unsnapped.

Up front, a musician
Used finger coition,
And while she was coming
From Wagner kept humming;
Then put in his wienie
To strains of Rossini,
And came to his glory
With *Il Trovatore*.

A young priest on her right
Sodomized her all night.
He came like a rabbit
And deplored his habit.

A judge seated in back
Took a leisurely whack,
And when done, said drolly,
"This'll hurt your parole."

A Frenchman 'cross the aisle
Watched it all with a smile,
And when each one was done,
Exclaimed, *"Vive le fun!"*

A young lad from first class
Stole a pinch of her ass.
He'll remember for weeks
Those soft velvety cheeks,
And forever, perchance,
How he came in his pants.

The stewardess rushed through,
"Coffee, tea, milk…or screw!"
But when she looked over
Those white breasts of Dover,
She gave out a loud scream
And containers of cream.

When the Captain came by
There was nought left to try.
He grumbled, "No joking,
There's been too much poking;
I'll turn off NO SMOKING,
And light up NO FOKING."
Now Wright knows what it means: *maiden flight.*

Will this meet the rigid standards of traditional limericists?
Is it simply too frilly? It certainly might be good fun if sung with
piano or guitar accompaniment, the first set of inner lines sung as
a solo, the second set as a duet, the third as a trio, the fourth as a

quartet, and so on. Then everyone could join in for the "fifth" line. The accompanist should add a *soupçon* of Wagner, Rossini, and the "Anvil Chorus" at the appropriate moment and feel free to embellish any of the sets as his genius sees fit. As far as we're concerned, this is a worthy challenge and we encourage dabblers to try their hands at the extended remix of the traditional limerick.

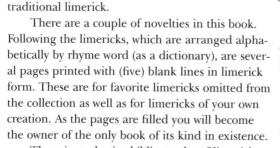

There are a couple of novelties in this book. Following the limericks, which are arranged alphabetically by rhyme word (as a dictionary), are several pages printed with (five) blank lines in limerick form. These are for favorite limericks omitted from the collection as well as for limericks of your own creation. As the pages are filled you will become the owner of the only book of its kind in existence.

There is a selective bibliography of limerick collections and a roll of honor of some of the composers included in this volume. To facilitate locating limericks, there is an index of the rhyme word of the fifth line (with the rhyme word of the first line in parentheses) for those who remember the fifth line only.

Thanks and appreciation go first of all to the master of limerick research, Gershon Legman, whose *The Limerick* is not only one of the largest but also perhaps the most carefully researched and annotated compilation; it has more than one hundred pages of notes and variants. It is the canon for all limericists. For all authors and editors of limericks, humble gratitude not only for their great personal contributions but also for the inspiration they have given over the years and the standards of excellence they have set. Since so many limericks are spread orally, it is not always possible to give credit and acknowledgment for every limerick. The editor and publisher offer sincere apologies to any authors whose limericks may have unintentionally been included in this volume without written or oral permission.

Finally, heartfelt thanks to the authors of the many original limericks in this collection, especially those who contributed them for the benefit of the readers of *Playboy*. May these worthy examples of the art be recited wherever limerick-lovers meet. And may new generations continue to carry high the great tradition of "accordion pleats full of airy conceits."

—Clifford Crist
New York City

ABSTENTION

A matron who favored abstention
Had breasts of unequal dimension.
When woo'd by her hubby,
She withheld the large bubby,
Thus causing domestic dissension.

ADA

A young taxidermist from Ada,
Whose wife said he'd often betrayed her,
Was sued for divorce
For mounting a horse,
A moose and a goose and a 'gator.

ADAIR

There was a young man named Adair
Who was having his girl on the stair.
When the banister broke,
He doubled his stroke,
And polished her off in mid-air.

ADAM

In the Garden of Eden lay Adam,
Caressing the mons of his madam;
    And he thought with elation,
    That in all of creation,
There were only two balls, and he had 'em.

ADROIT

Though at lying my aunt is adroit,
I don't see what she hopes to exploit
    By claiming a screw
    In Kalamazoo,
When I know it took place in Detroit.

AENOS

There was a young woman from Aenos
Who came to our party as Venus.
    We told her how rude
    'Twas to come in the nude,
And brought her a leaf from the green-h'us.

ALGIERS

There was an old bey of Algiers,
Who said to his harem, "My dears!
　　You may think it odd o' me,
　　But I've given up sodomy—
Tonight there'll be fucking!" (Loud cheers.)

ALICE

A gifted young tranny named Alice
Could pick up loose coins with her phallus,
　　But she couldn't make change,
　　Which narrowed her range
And kept her from playing the Palace.

ALICE

A sex-crazed nympho named Alice
Used a dynamite stick for a phallus.
　　They found her vagina
　　In North Carolina
And her asshole in Buckingham Palace.

ALSACE   There was a young man from Alsace,
Whose balls were constructed of brass.
        When he clanged them together,
        They played "Stormy Weather"
And lightning came out of his ass.
(And on Sundays, Bach's B Minor Mass.)

ALTHOUGH   Said a greedy old piggie, "Although
The sows leave when they've eaten enough,
        I still squat in the slough,
        With my snout in the trough;
I will never admit I am through."

ANCHOR   A sailor at Bangor cast anchor,
With syphilis, buboes, and chancre.
        All this, and some more,
        He'd got from one whore,
So he wrote her a letter to thank her.

ANDANTE CANTABILE

While humming "Andante Cantabile,"
A sculptor constructed a mobile.
    When it failed to revolve,
    He made this resolve:
"I really must build them more wobile."

ANHEUSER

There was a young girl named Anheuser,
Who boasted no man could surprise her.
    Pabst took a chance,
    Left Schlitz in her pants,
And now she is sadder Budweiser.

ARABIA

There was a young girl from Arabia,
Guilty of immodest behavia.
    She sat in each class,
    With her skirt round her ass,
Blowing kisses at the profs with her labia.

ARIES

A young lady born under Aries
Consults the stars each time she marries.
　　Although she gets hope
　　From each horoscope,
Her husbands have all turned out to be fairies.

ASGALUN

The monarch of old Asgalun
Behaved oddly at every full moon.
　　He would leap from his bed,
　　With his butt painted red,
And cry, "I'm a Kushite baboon!"

ASKEW

An old linotype went askew,
With its naked machinery in view.
　　In this state of undress,
　　It made love to the press,
Saying gently, "Etaoin shrdlu."

ASTOR There was a young woman named Astor,
Whose clothes fit her tighter than plaster.
        When she happened to sneeze,
        She felt a cold breeze,
And knew she had met with disaster.

ASTOR While befuddled with booze, Mr. Astor
Made a pass at a statue of plaster.
        When informed of his error,
        His mind filled with terror.
"What a blessing," he said, "I'm not faster."

A-TASKET When you think of "A-Tisket, A-Tasket,"
Remember the woman named Crasket,
        Who pulled a good stunt
        By rigging her front
And carrying her tits in a basket.

AUSTRALIA   There was a young man from Australia,
Who painted his bung like a dahlia.

> The drawing was fine,
> The color divine,

But the scent—well, that was a failia.

AVERY   There was an old bishop named Avery
Whose habits were highly unsavory.

> With devilish howls
> He deflowered young owls,

Which he kept in an underground aviary.

BABBIT   Two geneticists named Hansen and Babbit,
Crossed a small camel with a rabbit.

> The offspring was jumpy,
> And frightfully lumpy,

And had a lascivious habit.

BAD

A young man from Ward said, "Too bad,
There's nothing in sight but a lad.
    I'll just have to retrench
    On this yen for a wench,
But it does make me feel like a cad."

BÄGER

A German musician named Bäger,
Spurred on by a very high wager,
    Proceeded to fart
    The complete oboe part
Of a Haydn octet in A major.

BALL

It's my own fault I have just one ball,
And it's lucky I have one at all:
    I'm also cross-eyed
    And shouldn't have tried
To wear my poor cat as a shawl.

BANGOR

There was a young lady from Bangor,
Who slept while the ship lay at anchor.
    She awoke with dismay
    To hear the mate say,
"Let's lift up the top-sheet and spanker."

BARD

In the speech of his time, did the Bard
Refer to his prick as his "yard";
    But do not sigh, madams:
    'Twas no longer than Adam's
Or mine, and not one half so hard.

BARNARD

The eminent Christiaan Barnard,
Back when Viagara was a hopeless canard,
    Found, by transplanting epoxy
    Into older men's jocks, he
Could help them to get pretty hard.

BARODA   There was a young girl of Baroda,
Who built a new kind of pagoda.
    The walls of its halls
    Were hung with the balls
And the tools of the fools who bestrode her.

BARR   An undertaker named Barr
Took matters a little too far.
    When business was laggin',
    He took his black wagon
And started up Hearse Rent-a-Car.

BATES   There was a young lady named Bates,
Who was cursed from birth by the Fates.
    She wished that she could,
    And feared that she would,
And that was the end of her dates.

BATONGER

There was a young girl from Batonger,
Who was jazzing herself with a conger.
    When asked how it feels
    To be pleasured by eels,
She replied, "Like a man, only longer."

BAY HEAD

There was a young woman from Bay Head,
Who took a young man to her bed.
    She hoped her mons he would kiss,
    And so bring her to bliss,
But he read an old *Playboy* instead.

BEAL

A modest young lady named Beal
Protected herself with great zeal,
    So when she'd been wedded,
    The thing that she'd dreaded
Was a treat of enormous appeal.

BEERS Said a white-haired old lady named Beers,
As she balled with a quintet of queers,
"As God is my witness,
This is the shit'nest
Gang-bang I've had in nine years!"

BEGAT There was a young girl who begat
Triplets named Nat, Tat, and Pat.
It was fun in the breeding,
But hell in the feeding—
She found there was no tit for Tat.

BEGINNING God's plan had a hopeful beginning,
But man spoiled his chances by sinning.
We trust that the story
Will end in God's glory,
But, at present, the other side's winning.

BELGRAVIA   There was a young man from Belgravia,
Who cared neither for God nor his Saviour.
He would walk down the Strand
With his prick in his hand,
And be jailed for indecent behaviour.

BEN   A loopy young farmer named Ben,
Had lustful designs on a hen,
Who, rather than hide,
Most obligingly cried,
With a flip of her feathers, "Just say when!"

BETH   Screamed a muscular housewife named Beth,
As she choked her dumb husband to death,
"I've never found lipstick
Adorning your dipstick,
But that's sure FDS on your breath!"

BENARES   A nudist resort at Benares
Took a midget in, all unawares,
But he made members weep
For he just couldn't keep
His nose out of private affairs.

BENGAL   There was a young man of Bengal,
Who swore he had only one ball.
Then two little bitches,
They pulled down his britches—
And found that he had none at all!

BENGAL   There was a young man of Bengal
Who went to a fancy-dress ball.
Just for a whim,
He dressed up as a quim,
And was had by the dog in the hall.

BERLIN

There was a young girl in Berlin
Who had sex with an elderly Finn.
  Though he diddled his best
  And screwed her with zest,
She kept asking, "Hey, Pop! Is it in?"

BESS

A famous fellatrice named Bess
Refused all requests from the press
  To explain her renown
  As a great goer-down—
She was tight-lipped about her success!

BIG DELL

There was a young athlete, Big Dell,
Whose tool was too large for his belle.
  While the surgeon was clipping,
  The knife started slipping—
Now he's called by his friends Tinkerbell.

BILL   A medical marvel named Bill
Had a tool that was shaped like a quill.
  This remarkable dink
  Could squirt purple ink
And write, draw, or color at will.

BIRMINGHAM   There were two young ladies from Birmingham,
And this is the story concerning 'em.
  They lifted the frock,
  And played with the cock,
Of the bishop while he was confirming 'em.

But the bishop was nobody's fool;
He'd been sent to a large public school.
  So he pulled down his britches
  And skizzled the bitches
With his eight-inch Episcopal tool.

It is true that the bishop of Birmingham
Diddled these girls while confirming 'em.
  'Mid liturgical chants,
  He took down his pants
And released the Episcopal sperm in 'em.

This bishop did nothing amiss
In conducting these lasses to bliss.
    May the Church ne'er unfrock
    His Episcopal cock,
But keep it, a relic to kiss!

BLANCHE

There was a young lady named Blanche,
Who screwed all the boys at the ranch.
    After screwing all day
    'Til their pricks wore away,
She demanded nocturnal *revanche*.

BLUM

A most passionate spinster named Blum
Found a lad who was eager but dumb.
    With her hand on his knee,
    She said, "Come and see!"
He replied, "Don't you mean 'see and come'?"

BOAST   I confess that I'm not one to boast
Of orgiastic delights…but a toast:
    To the stupendous ability
    Of my once proud facility,
I think I remember…almost.

BOIST   A Brooklyn boy ready to boist,
Shacked up wit' a French goil, his foist.
    When she said, "Ah! *Mon cher!*"
    He replied, "Stop right dere!
Would you radder we fuckt or convoist?"

BOISTEROUS   There was a young abbess, too boisterous,
Who was sent off posthaste from the cloisters—
    She'd poured vichyssoise
    On the salade niçoise,
And Bavarian cream on the oysters.

BOMBAY

There was a young girl from Bombay
Who was put in a family way,
By the mate of a lugger,
A prolific young bugger,
With twelve kids in old Mandalay.

BOMBAY

There was a young man of Bombay,
Who constructed a woman of clay,
But the heat of his prick
Turned the clay into brick,
And he wore all his foreskin away.

BONE

There was a young dentist named Bone,
Who catered to ladies alone.
In a fit of depravity,
He filled the wrong cavity.
My God! How his business has grown!

BONHOMIE When Pan, full of classical bonhomie,
Met a maiden, she cried, "Don't get onna me!
    And the goats I keep, too,
    I forbid you to screw;
I have just read a book—Deuteronomy!"

BOOT 'Twas the thirteenth, and Friday to boot,
When he first wore his new Gucci suit.
    Before the next morn
    It was spotted and torn,
But his girl thought his root was still cute.

BORDEAUX A clumsy young clod from Bordeaux
Was jazzing a girl in St. Lô.
    They fell from her sack,
    He stepped on her crack,
Now he's nursing clap of the toe.

BOSTON

There was a young fellow from Boston,
Who drove around in an Austin.
    He had room for his ass,
    And a gallon of gas,
But his balls hung out—and he lost 'em.

BOUGH

A young writer of Verses named Bough
Ate the Loaf, drained the Jug, then yelled, "Thou
    Mak'st my life a total mess,
    Singing in the Wilderness,
Hush, love, thou'st spoiled Paradise enow."

BOULDER

A boastful blonde virgin from Boulder
Swore no man or boy had yet rolled her.
    She was therefore chagrined
    When photos of her sins
Appeared in the summer school folder.

BRACT

A young trapeze-swinger named Bract
Is faced by a very grim fact:
    Consider his pain
    When, again and again,
He catches his wife in the act.

BRAY

An indolent vicar of Bray
Spent before he withdrew, one fine day.
    His wife, quite alert,
    Felt the man's squirt,
And smirked to her spouse, "Let us spray!"

BRENDA

So well stacked was a freshman named Brenda,
Campus studs yearned to part her pudenda.
    They were all quite irate
    When her inaugrual date
Wasn't Tom, Dick, or Harry—but Glenda!

BRENT
There was a young lady named Brent
Who upon her divorce had this comment:
　　"Life had been fine,
　　And the sex was divine,
'Til my husband became indifferent!"

BRENT
There was a young woman of Brent
With a mons of enormous extent;
　　And so deep and so wide,
　　The acoustics inside
Were so good you could hear when you spent.

BRICE
A leprous old bastard named Brice
Had balls that were spotted like dice.
　　They couldn't make sperm
　　And were overly firm,
But made a wonderful gambling device.

BRIDGET

There was a young coed named Bridget,
Who dressed in the clothes of a midget.
    Everyone in the class
    Got a peek at her ass,
And she'd wink at the prof with her twidget.

BRIGHTON

There was a young fellow from Brighton,
Who thought he'd at last found a tight one.
    He said, "Oh, my love,
    It fits like a glove!"
She replied, "You're not in the right one."

BRUGES

There once was a duchess of Bruges,
Whose mons was exceedingly huge.
    Said the king, as he came,
    To this spirited dame,
"Mon Dieu! Aprés moi, le déluge."

BRUNO There once was a gaucho named Bruno,
Who said, "Screwing is all that I do know.
 A woman is fine,
 A sheep is divine,
But a llama! There's *numero uno!*"

BRYDE There was a fat lady of Bryde
Whose shoelaces once came untied,
 But she didn't dare stoop,
 For fear she would poop,
And she cried and she cried and she cried.

BRYERDER There was a young trucker named Bryerder,
Who met a good hooker and hired her
 To fuck between trucks,
 But to truck between fucks
Made him tireder and tireder and tireder.

BULGARIA

There was a young man of Bulgaria
Whose genitals couldn't be hairier.
    He proposed to Beth Sands,
    Who had scissors for hands,
To which she replied, "I'll take care o' ya."

BULGARIA

There once was a Queen from Bulgaria,
Whose bush had grown hairier and hairier;
    When a prince from Peru
    Settled in for a screw,
He had to search for a perch with a terrier.

BURSAR

There once was an indigent bursar
Whose flatulent wife was a curser,
    So when she would start
    To fume and to fart,
He would let the fart bitch...and vice versa!

BURUNDA
A barbarous critic from Burunda
Committed a grave social bulunda,
  By having emissions
  Before several Titians
In the Andrew J. Mellon rotunda.

BUSTER
An effete young sailor named Buster
Was equipped with ten pricks in a cluster.
  He could have an erection
  In any direction,
And afterwards serve as a duster.

BYNUM
A newlywed husband named Bynum
Asked his bride to please sixty-nine him.
  When she shook her head,
  He sighed and then said,
"Well, if we can't lick 'em, let's join 'em."

BYZANCE Theodora the queen of Byzance,
Is remembered for having hot pants.
    At one *soirée de luxe*
    She took on three dukes,
Two eunuchs, one ape, and four aunts.

CALCUTTA There was an old man of Calcutta,
Who had an unfortunate stutter.
    "I would like," he once said,
    "Some bub-bub-bub-bread
And some bub-bub-bub-bub-bub-bub-butter."

CANCER A zoophile, born under Cancer,
Joined up as a cavalry lancer,
    But he died of despair
    When his favorite mare
Was replaced by a motorized panzer.

CAPE   There was an old man of the Cape
Who buggered a Barbary ape.
　　Said the ape, "Sir, your prick
　　Is too long and too thick,
And something is wrong with the shape."

CAPE   There was a young man from Cape Hatteras,
HATTERAS   Who kept poking holes through the matteras.
　　He said, with a wail,
　　"It's me wife's narrow tail!
I'll have to get one with a fatter ass."

CAPE HORN   There was a young man from Cape Horn,
Who wished he had never been born.
　　And he wouldn't have been,
　　If his father had seen
That the end of the rubber was torn.

CAPRI   There was a young wench of Capri
Who happened to fall in the sea.
    Lured by her odor,
    A dolphin bestrode her,
And she emerged transfigured with glee.

CAROUSE   Two lovers went out to carouse,
Without sanction or marital vows.
    Their happiness complete,
    They had sex in the street,
Which caused a slight raising of brows.

CARR   There once was a kiddie named Carr
Who found a man laying his mar.
    Said he, with a snicker,
    As he watched the guy stick her,
"Ya do it much faster than par."

CASEY

"Since my sex is bisex," cried Casey,
"I've chosen a city that's racy!
    With its either-or zest,
    I get letters addressed
To WASHINGTON, D.C. and A.C.

CAWNPORE

There was a young man of Cawnpore
Whose tool was so awfully sore
    From slapping and rubbing,
    And pulling and drubbing,
It was useless for what it was for.

CHASE

Said an elegant widow named Chase,
To her friend, all decked out in lace,
    "The heat of this museum
    Titillates my perineum—
Pardon me while I pee in this vase."

CHESTER A young maiden got married in Chester;
Her mother, she kissed her and blessed her,
   And said, "You're in luck;
   He's a marvelous fuck.
I know, for I've had him in Leicester."

CHESTER There was a young lady of Chester
Who fell in love with a jester.
   Her breath came out hotly
   At sight of his motley,
But the head on his wand most impressed her.

CHICHESTER There was a young lady from Chichester
Whose beauty made saints in their niches stir.
   As she knelt during Mass,
   The shape of her ass
Made the bishop of Chichester's britches stir.

CHINA
There was a young preacher from China
Who loved boys but thought birds diviner.
> But he gets no tail;
> Because he's in jail,
Being charged with corrupting a mynah.

CITEAUX
A horny young monk of Citeaux
Used to cool his hot rod in the snow,
> But no matter how frigid,
> The thing remained rigid,
Popping off when it got two below.

CLAIR
There was a young lady named Clair,
Who possessed a magnificent pair.
> Or that's what I thought
> 'Til I saw one get caught
On a thorn and start losing air.

CLAIRE   Young Tom met a woman named Claire,
Who had never been diddled down there.
    She said, "Copulation
    Can result in gestation,
But I swear, now you're there, I don't care."

CLAIRE   A highway-patrol cop named Claire
Once screwed half the force on a dare;
    From the heat of this game,
    Her parts burst into flame,
So they nicknamed her Smokey the Bare!

CLARENCE   A remarkable fellow named Clarence
Learned self-control from his parents.
    With his wife in bed nude,
    He'd sit there and brood,
And practice the art of forbearance.

CLASS

Everyday in algebra class
Alfred eyed his neighbor's fine ass.
    But she put *ab* with *c*
    Coefficently
And figured out that she'd rather pass.

CLETUS

A speedy young halfback named Cletus
Told his team, "I'm afraid State will beat us,
    But I've got a date
    With their coach's mate—
For revenge I'll give her athlete's fetus!"

CLOISTER

As dull as the life of the cloister
(Except it's a little bit moister),
    Mutatis mutandum
    Non est disputandum,
There's no thrill in sex for the oyster.

CLUNG

A romantic attraction has clung
To a chap of whom damsels have sung,
    "He's the Scourge from the East,
    That lascivious beast
Who was known as Attila the Hung!"

CLYDE

There was a young lady from Clyde,
Who'd herself suddenly a bride.
    She had asked for protection
    From her boyfriend's erection,
But what he heard was, "Come on inside!"

COHN

A randy young sideman named Cohn
Tied his donicker to his trombone.
    Though improving his skills
    On glissandos and trills,
It utterly ruined his tone.

COLONEL

An old martinet of a colonel
Had a temper positively infernal.
　　It would cause him to howl
　　That he was a night owl
Whose wife's tastes ran to the diurnal.

COMMUNITY

In a lewd diplomatic community,
A charge claimed he screwed with impunity;
　　And he soon had a shock
　　From the embassy doc:
See, he lacked diplomatic immunity.

CONGEAL YA

Poor Hamlet! It's fit to congeal ya,
To see what a fate life can deal ya.
　　For what did him in
　　Was a prick in the skin,
When the prick should have been in Ophelia.

CONNAUGHT There was an old man of Connaught,
Whose prick was remarkably short.
    When he got into bed,
    His old woman said,
"That isn't a prick—it's a wart!"

CONVERSION In the midst of a Baptist conversion,
A preacher kept urgin' a virgin.
    When she finally gave in
    He said, "It's no sin,
As long as it's total immersion."

COOPER Said the doc to James Fenimore Cooper,
"Son, there's something gone wrong with your pooper.
    The Indians, I fear,
    Have attacked from the rear,
While you lay in inebriate stupor."

CORA   A liberated woman named Cora
Thinks wedlock a male-devised horror.
    It's *sub rosa* screwing
    That everyone's doing—
And she prefers richer to poorer!

CORELLI   There was a fat girl named Corelli
Whose breasts hung down past her belly.
    She enjoyed copulation
    With such animation
That she mashed all her partners to jelly.

COURSE   The race for the moon's run its course:
Men and women are going in force.
    Now when they embrace
    In the cold dark of space
They call what they do "outercourse."

COWARD   Sir Lancelot, never a coward,
Every maiden in Camelot scoured.
    He even went farther
    And lanced his man Arthur—
That's when knighthood was truly deflowered!

COX   Said an anxious young woman named Cox,
"On birth-control pills, wish a pox!
    I take them each day,
    Like the instructions say,
But they always fall out of my box!"

CRANDALL   An eclectic collector called Crandall
Acquired, with the aid of a vandal,
    The bottled remains
    Of John Maynard Keynes,
And the organ of George Frederick Handel.
(And from the left foot of Plato a sandal.)

CRATER
A crafty cartographer, Crater,
Is known as a well-hung young satyr.
    Why his testes alone—
    To such size are they grown—
Must be viewed in projection Mercator!

CRAWL
(after Robert Frost)
Since early spring I've crept at snailish crawl
To finish this stone fence good neighbors call
    Good. Now the winds the stately birches bend
    And I have miles to go before I end...
Someone there is who doesn't love a wall.

CRETE
A young ballerina from Crete
Offered stagehands all they could eat.
    When one asked for a ride,
    She declined and then sighed,
"That would ruin my Nutcracker Suite."

CREWE

A startled young maiden of Crewe
Found an elephant's wang in her stew.
Said the waiter, "Don't shout,
And wave it about,
Or the rest will be wanting one, too."

CREWS

The hard-on of sheepherder Crews
Was one that he just couldn't lose.
He'd no girls to assault
So perhaps one can't fault
His putting his dick to good ewes.

CRIBBS

There once was a fellow named Cribbs
Whose cock was so big it had ribs.
Every time he undressed,
His girlfriend confessed
She was grateful for getting first dibs.
(Though blowjobs required two bibs.)

CRIED

There was a young outlaw who cried
When he hadn't a boyfriend to ride.
    And as for his moll,
    She slept with a doll—
That's the true story of Bonnie and Clyde.

CROFT

There was a young vicar named Croft
Who played with his organ (and oft),
    But afraid of a lapse,
    If he played in the apse;
    Or the bishop might rave,
    If he played in the nave;
    Or that he might falter,
    If too near the altar;
    And afraid he'd be whipped,
    If he slipped in the crypt;
He transplanted it up to the loft.

LeRoy Neiman

CROFT

There was a young woman of Croft,
Who played with herself in a loft,
    For tools she used candles—
    They'd never cause scandals!—
And besides which, they never went soft.

CROWNED

Cried a young whacker-off, "I'll be crowned
As the champ when word gets around;
    I've convincingly showed
    That I'm first with my load!
I can beat any jerk, pound for pound!"

CROYDON

There was an old vicar of Croydon,
Whose cook was a regular hoyden.
    She would sit on his knees,
    While shelling the peas,
Or similar duties employed on.

CRUMM
Said a tender young fellow named Crumm,
While massaging his fiancée's bum,
    "My fingers, I know,
    Are where they should go—
But what has become of my thumb?"

CRUMM
A randy young woman named Crumm
Thought her lover too naif and dumb.
    She gave him no rest
    'Til he straddled her chest,
At which point they were both overcome.

CRUZ
A crusading lady named Cruz
Was highly advanced in her views.
    She once in a zoo
    Liberated a gnu,
And was lavishly praised by the *News*.

CRY

Said Betty Friedan with a cry,
"There are rights we won't be denied.
    I think you'll allow, sirs,
    That feminine trousers
Should all come equipped with a fly."

DAHLIA

There was a young lady named Dahlia
Whose bust was, in truth, utter failure.
    Later surgically blessed
    With a chest like Mae West,
She died happy of hypermammalia.

DALLAS

A team playing baseball in Dallas
Called the umpire "a shit" out of malice.
    While this worthy had fits,
    The team made eight hits
And a girl in the bleachers named Alice.

DALLAS A huge-organed woman in Dallas
Named Alice (quite starved for a phallus)
    Was *virgo intacto*,
    Because, *ipso facto*,
No phallus in Dallas fit Alice.

DARJEELING A lusty young surgeon from Darjeeling
Transplanted a cock to her ceiling.
    When she wanted to ball,
    It was no good at all,
But the dangle, she felt, was appealing.

DASH There once was a toddler named Dash
Who went from happy to sad in a flash.
    Things would be swell,
    Then he'd start to yell—
It seems consistency gave him a rash.

DE BRAY

At the Louvre with the Countess de Bray,
We spent the most wonderful day
    By sketching a penis
    On a painting of Venus,
And a beard on a nude by Monet.

DEE

A cute London streetwalker, Dee,
Declared she was changing her fee.
    First, she got a whole crown,
    Then her prices went down.
So did she.

DEL NORTE

There was a young wench in Del Norte,
Who liked to screw men over forty.
    She said, "It's too quick
    With a young feller's prick—
I like it to last and be warty."

DEPLORABLE

A virgin, whose tightness deplorable
Made regular sex seem too horrible,
    At last had to marry
    A gay chap named Larry
Who thought her behind was adorable.

DEPOSIT

Cohn said to his wife in Deposit,
"Tillie, now tell me, howzit
    When we get into bed
    You look over my head
And wink at the man in the closet?"

DES MOINES

A young couple who came from Des Moines
Went to motels to vibrate their loins.
    She would sit on her mate
    And start to gyrate,
While he fed the bed bags of coins.

DETECTIVE

To his wife said the sharp-eyed detective,
"Can it be that my eyesight's defective?
    Has the east tit the least bit
    The best of the west tit,
Or is it a trick of perspective?"

DETROIT

There was a young girl from Detroit
Who at fucking was very adroit.
    She could contract her vagina
    To a pinpoint or finer,
Or make it as big as a quoit.

The girl had a friend named Durand,
Whose cock could contract or expand.
    He could bugger a midge,
    Or the arch of a bridge—
Their performance together was grand.

DEVIZES

There was a young man of Devizes
Whose balls were of different sizes.
    One was so small
    It weighed nothing at all;
But the other won numerous prizes.

DEVON

There was a young lady from Devon
Attacked in a thicket by seven
    Anglican priests—
    Libidinous beasts!—
Of such is the kingdom of heaven.

DICE

There was a young fellow from Dice,
Who remarked, "I think bigamy's nice.
    Even two are a bore;
    I prefer three or four!
For the plural of spouse is 'spice.'"

DIME
When a hooker cost only a dime,
A guy could get laid all the time
  When it went up to twelve bucks
  For a couple of fucks,
It was the start of organized crime.

DIMMER
This one guy, who couldn't be dimmer,
One day had the tiniest glimmer,
  Of what life would be like,
  Had his dad rode a bike,
Instead of his mom's ample quimmer.

DINED
It was after the couple had dined
That the fellow began to unwind,
  Said he, "I like you, Regina,
  You think with your vagina!"
Then she gave him a piece of her mind.

DISCARD Up in Sing Sing the wardens discard
Any pretense of being on guard.
> Though the convicts deny it,
> Their saltpeter diet
Makes it hard to get hard in the yard.

DON QUIXOTE Raise sabres! Salute Don Quixote!
A hero most raunchy and goaty.
> As his fleshy pink lance
> Put the young man in a trance,
He explained, "I don't normally go in for this
> sort of thing, leaning strongly as I do
> toward heterosexual rather than homosexual in
> matters pertaining to delights of the flesh...
But, you see, I am high on peyote!"

DOOM

Possessed by a demon of doom,
The man screwed a ghost in Khartoum.
  He did it, they say,
  In the regular way
(Under the sheets, we presume).

DOREEN

There's a sophomore at State named Doreen
Who's renowned on the oral-sex scene.
  Since vibrato, it's said,
  Is the crown on her head,
She's been voted the Humcoming Queen.
(Three times running since turning sixteen!)

DORIS

A comely young cavegirl named Doris
Made love to a male brontosaurus.
  She exclaimed, "For a word
  To explain what occurred,
I'd have to consult a thesaurus."

DOT

Said the young gardener Dot,
"There's something I ponder a lot:
    If I water my bush,
    And prune it when lush,
Will that prevent the onset of rot?"

DOW

There was an old farmer named Dow,
Who said, "I feel wonderful now;
    They've transplanted the tongue,
    A section of lung,
And the pituitary gland from *mmmmmmmy* cow."

DOYLE

A hot-blooded swordsman named Doyle
Didn't fence quite "according to Hoyle."
    When challenged to duel,
    He'd whip out his tool,
And brandish it about like a foil.

DRAKE UNIVERSITY

Said a student from Drake University,
When asked about sexual diversity,
  "While a lay is O.K.
  In the regular way,
I *prefer* polymorphous perversity."

DREAM

Sheba's queen was King Solomon's dream,
Though their love life was not what 'twould seem:
  For in olden days
  They washed not for days,
And smelled like a broken latrine.

DRIFT

It had snowed, and the man in the drift
Flagged her down and requested a lift;
  As they say in her Bentley,
  She fondled him gently—
And that lift that he'd asked for was swift!

DROLL
A girl for a caddy is droll;
After golf, you may give her a roll.
    But by night, as by day,
    She's as likely to say,
"Sir, you are playing the wrong hole."

DUD
Hot roast fowl can end up a dud,
Worse than *remoulade* over mud.
    When in chef's cap or capote,
    Serving a great *table d'hôte*,
We always serve pressed duck in cold blood.

DULUTH
A hasty young man from Duluth
Phoned back home to his sweetheart, Ruth.
    When he made the connection
    He got an erection—
Then lost it right there in the booth.

DULUTH

There was an old maid of Duluth,
Who wept when she thought of her youth,
    Remembering chances
    She'd missed at school dances,
And once in a telephone booth
With a "lithpy" young man, name of "Brooth."

DUNDEE

(To Winston Churchill)

A young man once went to Dundee,
And addressing the voters, said he,
    "No house is complete
    Unless I have a seat;
My initials are W.C."

DUNDEE

There was an old man of Dundee,
Who came home as drunk as could be.
    He wound up the clock
    With the end of his cock,
And screwed his poor wife with the key.

DUNDEE

There was a young man from Dundee,
Who screwed a baboon in a tree.
    The offspring was horrid,
    All ass and no forehead,
Three balls and a purple goatee.

DUNELLEN

A rosy-cheeked lass from Dunellen,
Whom the Hoboken sailors called "Helen,"
    In her efforts to please,
    Spread venereal disease
From New York to the Straits of Magellan.

DURANGO

An innocent maid of Durango
Wasn't told where to make a man's wang go,
    But she acquired this knowledge
    Her first night in college,
With a musical sigh like a tango.

DUTTON

There was a young fellow named Dutton,
Whose balls were the size of a button,
He did have a dong
Some twelve inches long,
But what could he do with it? Nuttin'.

EAST BAINBRIDGE HALL

A student of East Bainbridge Hall
Had an organ exceedingly small.
He buggered a bug
On the edge of the rug,
But the bug didn't feel it at all.

EAST BIRMINGHAM

Lady Eva of East Birmingham
Got herself in a terrible jam.
While succumbing to lust,
She put too much trust
In the fit of a friend's diaphragm.

EAST LYNNE
There was a young girl of East Lynne
Whose mother, to save her from sin,
 Had tied 'round her waist
 A titanium brace,
But the boy from the smithy got in.

ELATED
A Cherokee maid was elated
To think that she soon would be mated.
 She was asked how she knew
 That her brave's love was true;
Cried the maiden, "The buck is inflated!"

ELIAS
There was a young girl named Elias,
Whose panties were cut on the bias.
 There was also a loop,
 Through which she could poop,
And conjugate with her boyfriend Tobias.

ELLIS   A gung-ho marine, Sergeant Ellis,
With *esprit de corps* much too zealous,
    Drilled his penis to stand
    At the sound of the band,
While his anus blew *Semper Fidelis*.

EMPORIUM   The new xxx film emporium
Is by no means just a sexorium,
    But a highly effectual,
    And ambisexual,
Mutual masturbatorium.

ERSKINE   There was a young lady of Erskine,
Who had some remarkable ferskine.
    When I said to her, "Mabel,
    You look hot in your sable,"
She said, "I really look best in my berskine."

ETON

There was a young lady of Eton,
Whose bottom had plenty of meat on.
   She said, "Marry me, Jack,
   And you'll find that my back-
Side's good for more than finding a seat on."

EUTOXETER

There was a young girl from Eutoxeter,
So hot the boys pushed their cocks at her.
   From one of the jocks
   She contracted the pox,
And, in turn, poxed all the cocks in Eutoxeter.

EVA

A sexy young woman named Eva,
Went to a ball as Mrs. Cleaver,
   When a change in the lights
   Showed a rent in her tights,
Someone cried, "There's June Cleaver's beaver!"

EXETER
There was a young lady of Exeter,
So pretty that men craned their necks at her.
    One was even so brave
    As to take out and wave
The distinguishing mark of his sex at her.

FARM
A girl who came East from the farm
Exclaimed, "City life has its charm.
    Take the pleasures of orgasm,
    Every girl in New York has 'em,
But in Kansas they're viewed with alarm."

FASHION
There was a young woman of fashion,
Who had oodles and oodles of passion.
    To her lover she said,
    As they piled into bed,
"This is one thing those bastards can't ration!"

FAYE

A female biologist, Faye,
Hopes that parthenogenesis may
    One day sever the nexus
    Between the two sexes.
And make the men of the world fade away!

FEAR

A man with venereal fear
Had intercourse in his wife's ear.
    She said, "I don't mind,
    Except that I find
When the telephone rings, I can't hear."

FÊTE

At a rather too elegant fête,
Where a large group of freaks arrived late,
    A cunnilingulate whore
    And a queer from Mysore
Were engaged in bizarre tête-à-tête.

FEW

When the clients are more than a few,
There's a savvy old madam named Drew
    Who'll establish a line
    By displaying a sign
That informs all arrivals: FUCK QUEUE.

FIFE

A mortician who practiced in Fife
Made love to the corpse of his wife.
    "How would I know, Judge?
    She was cold, did not budge—
Just the same as she'd acted in life!"

FINE

While computer advances are fine,
It's the jargon involved that I mind:
    When we see one machine
    Spoon with another, does it mean
It's engaged in 1000110100100 or 69?

FLO "Though you paid me up front," hooker Flo
Told her client, "I'm still due some dough,
    I felt in gradations,
    Eleven pulsations,
And I quoted you ten bucks a throe."

FLOCK After scolding his penitent flock,
The pontiff exhorted his cock,
    "You pendulous shrimp,
    You just dangle there limp;
You're supposed to be Peter—a rock!"

FLOOD A dynamic young cocksman named Flood
Who was thinking of standing at stud,
    Had his instrument nipped
    By some dentures that slipped—
His career had been nipped in the pud.

FLORENCE

There was a young woman of Florence,
So lewd she used lube in great torrents.
   She said, "If he's small,
   I don't mind at all—
It's abstinence I view with abhorrence!"

**FLORIDA
KEYS**

An ecologist from the Florida Keys,
Said, "We'll solve water pollution with ease.
   Widespread constipation
   Can save our poor nation—
We must all live on alum and cheese!"

FLUTE

A tutor who tooted the flute
Tried to tutor two tutors to toot.
   Said the two to the tutor,
   "Is it harder to toot, or
To tutor two tutors to toot?"

FLYNN

There was a young lady named Flynn,
Who thought fornication a sin,
But when she was tight
She thought it alright,
So everyone plied her with gin.

FORMIA

There was a young woman of Formia
Whose housekeeping ways would disarm ya.
When there came a cold snap,
She'd climb in your lap,
So her little base-burner could warm ya.

FORSOOTH

A sperm faced, alack and forsooth,
His moment of sexual truth!
He'd expected to fall
On a womb's spongy wall,
But was fatally crushed on a tooth.

FORT KNAPP

There was a young man from Fort Knapp
Who boasted a cock full of sap.
    He said, with a snigger,
    "It gets bigger and bigger,
Or, shit, maybe it's only the clap...."

FRAIL

On the breast of a whore young and frail
Was tattooed the price of her tail,
    And on her behind,
    For the sake of the blind,
Was the very same thing, but in Braille.

FRANCE

An exchange student stationed in France
Let Frenchmen galore in her pants.
    "At home," she once said,
    "We do it in bed,
But here it's a matter of chance."

FRANCE   A pretty young maiden of France
Decided she'd take just one chance.
　　She let herself go
　　And bedded her beau,
And now all her sisters are aunts.

FRANCE   A young Vassar student from France
Had a lover with St. Vitus dance.
　　It was awkward, no doubt,
　　When they were out and about,
But was grand when he got in her pants.

FRANCE
(A rare three-liner)

There was a young fellow from France
Who waited ten years for his chance.
Then he blew it.

FREED

In a gay theater troupe, actor Freed
Was consumed by a cocksucking need.
When they found him in bed
With the star, the man said,
"It's a game where I'm blowing the lead!"

FREI

Said an aged Madrid cocksman named Frei,
"I refuse these new fashions to try.
Why, every zipper
Is like Jack the Ripper!
I shall stick to my old Spanish fly."

FRIGHTFUL   The harlots in London are frightful,
And the queens—those fey bastards—are spiteful!
    But I'm not in a heat,
    For I happened to meet
A sheep in Hyde Park. 'Twas delightful.

FRYE   An aging professor named Frye,
Who yearned to swap wives but was shy,
    Had a colleague named Klein
    Who suggested, "Try mine"—
And so began the "old college try."

FUN   A beach bum who loved to have fun
Was screwing his girl in the sun.
    His poor ass, being bare,
    Was cooked medium rare,
But his girl kept insisting, "Well done!"

FYFE

A despairing old landlord named Fyfe,
With a frigid and quarrelsome wife,
    Let his third-story flat
    To a hooker named Pat,
Who supplied him a new lease on life!

GABLE

A wood-fetish busboy named Gable
Is rapid, is thorough, is able;
    But when everything's cleared,
    He gives way to the weird
As he lovingly busses each table.

GALL

A disqualified wrestler with gall,
As a woman had fooled one and all.
    Said she, with a scream,
    "I'd have made the men's team,
If they'd only transplanted one ball!"

GAMBETTA   A filthy young man named Gambetta
Liked whores but thought he could do better;
    He took out an ad:
    "Wanted: girls gone bad.
Please list your sins in your letter."

GAMBETTA   A handsome Italian, Gambetta,
Once used an imperfect French letter;
    But the story gets worse,
    With the clap he was cursed,
And it took a long time to get better.

GATES   There was a young sailor named Gates,
Who got along well with his mates,
    'Til he fell on a cutlass,
    Which rendered him buttless,
And practically useless on dates.

GAY

There once was a pope who was gay;
He would ride down the Appian Way
 And wink at the ladies
 From his little Mercedes,
Which he'd nicknamed the "Auto da Fé."

GENDER

"I should like," said my aunt, "to change gender.
Every part of me's bruised, torn, and tender,
 For me man weighs a ton—
 Six times nightly has fun!—
And in short is a damned heavy spender."

GENOA

There was a young man from Genoa,
Whose prick was two inches, no moa.
 It was all right for pissing,
 For nothing was missing,
But it brought smiles to the lips of his whoa.

GHENT

There was a young fellow from Ghent,
Whose cock was so long that it bent.
    To save himself trouble,
    He put it in double,
And instead of coming, he went!

GHERRITY

There was a young widow named Gherrity,
Who said, with mordant asperity,
    "I'd have cut off his dilly
    To use occasionally,
Had he not willed the thing to a charity."

GINGERY

A young lad with passions quite gingery
Tore a hole in his sister's best lingerie.
    He pinched her behind,
    And made up his mind
To add incest to insult and injury.

GIOTTO

An Italian painter named Giotto
Seduced a nun in a grotto.
　　The result of his crime
　　Was two boys at one time;
"Give your sons to the church," was his motto.

GLAZE

A Cordon Bleu Charlotte named Glaze
Makes *hors d'oeuvres* that truly amaze.
　　When the men in her classes
　　Boldly make passes,
She gives them all straight *bordelaise*.

GLENGARRY

There was a young man of Glengarry,
Whose cock was too heavy to carry.
　　So he put it on wheels
　　And hired trained seals
To pull him around Londonderry.

GLORIA   There was a young hooker named Gloria,
Who was had by Sir Gerald du Maurier,
    And then by six men,
    Sir Gerald again,
And the band at the Waldorf Astoria.

GLOUCESTER   There was a young girl from Gloucester
Whose parents thought they had lost her.
    But they found in the grass
    The marks of her ass
And the knees of the man who had crossed her.

GLUM   I was feeling considerably glum;
Being cursed with a too-active bum.
    Said my doc, "For your Wheaties,
    Substitute cantharides,
Then, instead of going, you'll come."

GOFF

A vasectomy surgeon named Goff
Says that drinkers would probably scoff,
　　But the pleasure has gone
　　From his tying one on—
He prefers to be tying one off!

GORE

Theological student Tom Gore,
While using his fist for a whore,
　　Said, "It's no substitute
　　For a good prostitute,
But I can always come back for more."

GORING

There was a young fellow from Goring,
Who made a small hole in the flooring.
　　He lined it all round,
　　Then laid on the ground,
And declared it was cheaper than whoring.

GOSSAL

A young geologist from Gossal
Discovered a fossil colossal.
 He could tell by the bend,
 And the knob on the end,
'Twas the peter of Paul the Apostle.

GRACE

A Bennington student named Grace
Slipped a barbed-wire pessary in place.
 Her ethics professor
 Bent down to caress her,
And for his sins wound up losing face.

GRACE

In the midst of an anthem of grace,
The choirmaster slipped from his place
 To goose the soprano
 In a lingering manner,
Then returned with a smile on his face.

GRANT

There was a young fellow named Grant,
Whose good looks caused women to pant.
   When asked, "Do you fuck?"
   He replied, "No such luck;
I would if I could but I can't."

GREECE

That saucy old Sappho of Greece,
Said once, when mentoring her niece,
   "I like my pudenda
   Rubbed hard by the enda
The tongue of my girlfriend, Berniece."

GREELY

A freelancing artist named Greely
Had a model that suited ideally.
   At the first scent of paint,
   She would fall in a faint,
And only revived when lanced freely.

GREEN

There was a young lady named Green,
Who grew so abnormally lean,
    And flat, and compressed,
    That her back touched her chest,
And sideways she couldn't be seen.

GREEN BAY

A tackle who played for Green Bay
Was in training each night and each day.
    Isometric coition
    May improve one's condition,
But isn't as much fun in that way.

GREENWICH

There was a young fellow from Greenwich
Who lived on nothing but speenwich.
    It lengthened his tool,
    Which he kept on a spool,
'Til he unwound it, eenwich by eenwich.

GRESSION　A large-breasted Bunny named Gression
Sold cigars at a Key Club concession.
　　When she swiveled about,
　　Even strong men cried out,
For her costume did not keep her flesh in.

GRIMES　There was a young woman named Grimes,
Who spent all her nickels and dimes
　　On satin and lace
　　To hold her in place
And keep her abreast of the times.

GROUCH　Winter makes me feel like a grouch;
I cough and I sneeze and I slouch,
　　And I can't go canoeing
　　To get in my screwing,
Though a lot can be done on the couch.

HACK

There once was a lexicon hack
Unemployable because of his lack
    Of grammatical knowledge;
    (He'd spent most of college
Conjugating all day in the sack.)

HALTING

In Sodom, great feasts knew no halting,
And Lot was the guest they all called in.
    Said each host, "We love you,
    But your wife must come, too;
The stew is too flat and needs salting."

HANDEL

There was a musician named Handel
Whose intimate life was a scandal.
    When he fugued his bass
    He grew red in the face
And buggered himself with a candle.

HANG

"Dear Susan, I don't give a hang,"
Wrote the man to his ex-wife in Danang.
    "But here is the thing:
    If you don't have my ying,
What the fuck will you do with your yang?"

HANNAH

A prissy old maid named Miss Hannah
Wrote Burbank a note in this manner:
    "Could you spare a few hours
    From your shrubs and your flowers
And put a pulse in the banana?"

HARE

A clever young surgeon named Hare
Told *Time* what he'd done on a dare.
    "I gave a lobotomy
    To twin hippopotami.
Now one of them's running for mayor."

HARRIDGE　There was a young lady of Harridge,
　　　　　Who said, on the morn of her marriage,
　　　　　　　　"I shall sew my chemise
　　　　　　　　Right down to my knees;
　　　　　I refuse to be fucked in the carriage."

HARROW　A hopeful young fellow from Harrow
　　　　　Once feathered his cock like an arrow.
　　　　　　　　"There's room for improvement,"
　　　　　　　　Said his girl, "in the movement.
　　　　　Make it flutter about like a sparrow."

HARROW　There was a young lady of Harrow
　　　　　Who thought her vagina too narrow.
　　　　　　　　For times without number
　　　　　　　　She would use a cucumber,
　　　　　But could never quite manage a marrow.

HARWICH

There was a young parson of Harwich,
Tried to grind his betrothed in a carriage.
    She said, "No, you young goose;
    Just try self-abuse,
And the other we'll do after marriage."

HASDRUB-BABLE

There was a young man named Hasdrubbable,
Who had one real and one rubber ball.
    His young wife was odd, too:
    Through surgery and glue,
She had one rubber bub and one rubbable.

HATCH

There was a young lady named Hatch
Who had a rectangular snatch,
    So she practiced coition
    With a mathematician
Who had a square root to match.

HATCH

There was a young lady named Hatch,
Who said, "I just adore Bach;
    He isn't so fussy
    As Brahms or Debussy;
Sit down, and I'll play you a snatch."

HAVANA

A deep baritone from Havana,
While singing, slipped on a banana.
    He was ill for a year,
    Then resumed his career
As an oversized lyric soprano.

HAYES

A patient young Girl Scout named Hayes
Rubbed two fagots together for days,
    'Til she happened to pass
    A bubble of gas,
Which kindled a wonderful blaze.

HE

So dextrous a doctor was he,
His technique was something to see.
    'Til nurse Dowd, a virgin,
    Cried out, "Oh, my surgeon!
You poked the wrong organ in me!"

HEARST

A notorious whore named Miss Hearst
In the pleasures of men is well versed.
    Reads a sign o'er the head
    Of her oft-rumpled bed:
"The customer always comes first."

HECTOR

Cried a kinky young barber named Hector,
Who'd depantied a girl to inspect her:
    "I sure hope you don't care
    If I clip off some hair—
For, you see, I'm a boxtop collector."

HELEN

The breasts of a woman named Helen
Were the size of a large watermelon.
  When she hove into sight,
  All the boys would take fright
And run away, screamin' and yellin'.

HENTY

"I enjoy," claimed a nympho named Henty,
"Having sex with fifteen or twenty.
  And the sessions I prize
  Have a surfeit of guys
For an orgy's a horny of plenty!"

HERNIA

There was a young girl with a hernia,
Who said to her doctor, "Gol dern ya!
  When slicing my middle,
  I pray do not fiddle
With matters that do not concern ya."

HERO

For the next Games' finale, the hero
Gets a crack at the empress' zero,
    While the emperor stands by
    Swinging out *Träumerei*
On his flame-throwing fiddle.
        Signed,
        Nero.

HETERA

A lady stockbroker, quite hetera,
Decided her fortunes to bettera.
    On the floor, quite unclad,
    She successively had
Merrill Lynch, Goldman Sachs, et cetera.

HIGH   Said the truck driver, shifting to high,
And stroking his passenger's thigh,
"Inside my valise
Are some rubbers and grease;
Let's open them up, bye and bye."

HILARY   There was a young soldier named Hilary
Who spent sev'ral days in the pillory.
Reconnoit'ring a lass,
He had reached such a pass
That he brought up his heavy artillery.

HILDA   There was a young lady named Hilda
Who had the hots for a builder.
She told him he could,
And he said that he would;
But in the end he used a big dilda.

HIPPED

A gal from L.A. who was hipped
Went out to the beach to get dipped.
  She had on a Jantzen,
  But only the pants, 'n
She found herself at Sunset, stripped.

HITCHIN

There was a young fellow named Hitchin
Who was screwing the maid in the kitchen.
  In the midst of their lovin'
  He backed into the oven
And woke up the house with his bitchin'.

HOHOKUS

A cameraman from Hohokus
Photographed the mayor in focus.
  The shot that he got
  Put the boss on the spot:
Six aldermen mere kissing his tokus.

HOHOKUS A magician who hailed from Hohokus
Found his act an exciting new focus
  When two girl volunteers
  Triggered audience cheers
By insisting, "First hocus—then poke us!"

HOLLIS A hillbilly farmer named Hollis
Used possums and snakes for his solace.
  The children had scales
  And prehensile tails
And he developed an unholy callous.

HOOPLE There was a young maiden named Hoople
Whose bosom was triple, not duple.
  She had one removed,
  But it grew back, improved;
At present, Miss Hoople's quadruple.

HOORAY
Shouted Frosty the Snowman, "Hooray!"
I'm agog with excitement today!
    And the reason, of course:
    A reliable source
Said a snow blower's heading this way!"

HOWARD
Full of lust, a swim teacher, Bill Howard,
Was screwing a girl while she showered.
    He told her, "I hope
    You're still holding the soap,
Or else it's the Lux I've deflowered."

HUAN
A wise Chinese druggist named Huan
Was awarded a prize by the khan
    For a sexual depressive
    To calm thoughts obsessive,
Though it involves frequent trips to the john.

HUGHES

There was an old fellow named Hughes,
Who swore off on all kinds of booze.
    Said he, "When I'm muddled,
    My senses get fuddled,
And I pass up too damn many screws."

HYDE

Rued ex-Bunny, Miss Winifred Hyde,
"Most men don't like being denied."
    When asked, "What's to be done,
    When a man wants his fun?"
"They can play with themselves," she replied.

ILLUSION

Said a Spaniard, with little illusion,
As he felt on his head a contusion,
    "The thugs from South Spain
    Are not only a pain,
They are also a snare Andalusian!"

IMPERFECTIONS

A real-estate man's imperfections
As a lover caused female rejections.
    "I'm deflated," he moaned,
    "They're erogenous-zoned,
But only for high-rise erections."

IRAQ

There was a young man from Iraq,
Who played the bass viol with his cock.
    With tremendous erections,
    He could perform selections
From Johann Sebastian Bach.

ISTHMUS

There was a young man from the Isthmus
Whose bride had acute *vaginismus*.
    They found themselves stuck
    On the very first fuck,
And had to stay that way until Christmas.

JACQUES

A painter of Pop, known as Jacques,
Intends each new canvas to shock.
    Outsized genitalia
    Gave the critics heart-failia,
But one dubbed it pure Poppycock.

JAM

On the ark there was soon a great jam,
So Noah ate much veal and young lamb.
    'Course the taboos on pig
    Made that meat *infra dig*,
Though in secret Noah sometimes ate Ham.

JANUS

A noted torero named Janus
Was censored for conduct quite heinous.
    He was told, "On the bull
    Use your sword, *not* your tool,
And aim for the neck, not the anus."

JAPAN　Some women who live in Japan
Exist just for pleasing a man.
　　They'll give him fellatio,
　　Or a lay on the patio,
Or even a goose with a fan.

JAPAN　There was a young man of Japan
Whose limericks never would scan.
　　When someone asked why,
　　He would slowly reply,
"Perhaps it's because I always try to get as many
　　dirty words in the last line as I possibly can."

There was another young fellow from China
Whose sense of verse was much finer.
　　He thought it divine
　　To end the last line
Quite suddenly.

JOAN   There was a young lady named Joan
Who got all her thrills from the phone,
   Secreting the bell,
   And receiver as well,
Where you wouldn't believe, if not shown.

JUDE   There once was a woman named Jude
Who was such an insufferable prude
   That she pulled down the blind
   When changing her mind,
Lest a curious eye should intrude.

KANNEL   When they probed a young woman named Kannel,
Who complained she felt choked in her channel,
   They found shoehorns and spoons,
   Several busted balloons,
And twenty-two yards of red flannel!

KATE　　A beautiful maiden named Kate
Reclined in the dark with her date.
　　　When asked how she fared,
　　　She said she was scared,
But otherwise doing just great.

KAY　　A protesting teenager, Kay,
Joined a crowd one cold winter's day.
　　　She chanted out loud,
　　　With the antiwar crowd—
Until she got carried away.

KAY　　Ephraim and his crusading Kay
Love to picket by night and by day.
　　　They walk the same line
　　　And hold up a sign
That shows where you see Eph you see Kay.

KEATING

There was a poor fellow of Keating,
Whose pride took a terrible beating.
    That happens to males
    When they learn the details
Of their wives' extramarital cheating.

KELLY

There was a young couple named Kelly,
Who were stuck tight, belly to belly.
    It seemed, in their haste,
    They'd used library paste,
Instead of petroleum jelly.

KENT

There was a young woman from Kent
Who was sure she knew what it meant
    When he asked her to dine—
    Private room, lots of wine—
She knew—*Oh, she knew!*—But she went.

KENT

Three elderly spinsters of Kent
Gave up copulation for Lent.
    This included door handles,
    All tapers and candles,
And anything else that was bent.

KENT

Oh, pity the Dutchess of Kent!
Her vagina's so dreadfully bent,
    The poor wench doth stammer,
    "I need a sledgehammer
To pound a man into my vent."

KEW

A hermaphrodite swinger from Kew
Offered boys something new in a screw.
    Young men found it sweet
    On the front *and* back seat
Of this bisexual built just for two!

KEW

Said a lusty young maiden of Kew,
"I don't smoke, I don't drink, I don't chew.
　　But do not think, therefore,
　　There's nothing I care for,
If you know what I mean...and I'm pretty
　　damn sure that you do."

KEW

There was a young lady of Kew
Who said, as the curate withdrew,
　　"I prefer the dear vicar;
　　He's longer and thicker.
And besides, he comes quicker than you."

KHARTOUM

A gay man who lived in Khartoum
Took a lesbian up to his room.
　　They argued all night
　　Over who had the right
To do what, and with which, and to whom.

KHARTOUM   There was an old man of Khartoum,
Who kept a small goat in his room.
   "It reminds me," he stated,
   "Of a woman I dated,
But I can't recall exactly of whom."

KHIEF   There was an old abbot of Khief,
Who thought the Impenitent Thief
   Had bollocks of brass
   And an amethyst ass;
He died in this awful belief.

KILDARE   There was a young man from Kildare
Who was screwing a girl in a chair.
   At the sixty-third stroke,
   The furniture broke,
And his rifle went off in the air.

KILKENNY   There was an old whore of Kilkenny
Whose usual charge was a penny.
  For just half of that sum
  You could roger her bum—
A source of amusement to many.

KING   The last time I dined with the king,
He did a remarkable thing;
  As he sat on the stool
  And fondled his tool,
He remarked, "If I play, will you sing?"

KING'S   There was a young fellow of King's,
Who was weary of women and things.
  Said he, "My desire
  Is a boy from the choir,
With an ass that's like Jell-O on springs."

KING'S BLUFF

There was an old whore of King's Bluff,
Who said, "I have had quite enough
    Of men who are thirty,
    And forty and fifty;
What I need is that greasy kid stuff."

KIP

An obese old broker named Kip
Took a very fat girl on a trip.
    He was talking of stock,
    As he put in his cock.
At the end, she said, "Thanks for the tip."

KNEW

An anonymous woman we knew
Was dozing one day in her pew.
    When the preacher yelled, "Sin!"
    She said, "Count me in,
As soon as the service is through."

KRESS

For his concert, a flautist named Kress
Was in such a great hurry to dress,
    That on a high run
    His fly came undone,
And his organ got raves in the press.

KROCH

A cheerful young golfer named Kroch
Gave his tee shot a hundred-yard sock.
    It doesn't sound far
    For the man who shoots par,
But 'twas done with the end of his cock.

KROLL

A corpulent maiden named Kroll
Had a notion exceedingly droll;
    At a masquerade ball,
    Dressed in nothing at all,
She backed in as a Pillsbury roll.

KVETCH   A harlot who was an old kvetch
Came nine times with a well-endowed wretch.
Then, with prick 'twixt her thighs,
She declared, between sighs,
"I'd call this the tenth-inning stretch."

KYLE   An outrageous young lady named Kyle
Likes to flirt in a whimsical style:
She'll depanty, it's said,
And stand on her head
To display the most quimsical smile.

**LADY
NORRIS**   "'Tis my custom," said dear Lady Norris,
"To beg lifts from the drivers of lorries.
When they get out to piss,
I see things that I miss
At the wheel of my two-seater Morris."

LA JOLLA

There is an old man of La Jolla,
With a habit that's sure to anolla.
> Before telling a joke,
> He'll give you a poke,
And remark, "This one'll really destrolla!"

LAKE

Said a lovely young maiden named Lake,
Most unnaturally fond of a snake,
> "If my good friend, this boa,
> Shoots spermatozoa,
What offspring we'll leave in our wake!"

LAMAR

There's a buxom young wench in Lamar,
Whose shape is too nubile by far.
> One luscious bazoom
> Fills up half the room,
And the other's the size of a car.

LANCELOT   There was a young fellow named Lancelot
Whom the neighbors all looked at askance a lot,
  For whenever he'd pass
  A comely young lass,
The front of his pants would advance a lot.

LAND   Moaned Tessie, the whore, "In this land,
I've met bastards who thought it was grand
  To retire, when inclined,
  With sex problems in mind,
And awake with solution in hand."

LAPP   There was a young lecher named Lapp
Who thought condoms were so much crap.
  Said he, "All us he-men
  Like to scatter our semen."
Ten weeks later, he still has the clap.

LARKS

Said a woman on one of her larks,
"It's more fun indoors than in parks.
    You feel more at ease,
    Your ass doesn't freeze,
And strollers don't make snide remarks."

LARS

In Rome, a curator called Lars
Found, preserved in a cache of old jars,
    The cunny of great Venus,
    Old Jupiter's penis,
And, he *thinks,* the left knocker of Mars.

LASS

There was an eccentric young lass
Who wore panties constructed of brass.
    Said she, "They have uses,
    Like staving off gooses,
And pinches and pains in the ass."

LAST   An emasculate lad said, "At last,
I've an elephant trunk for a mast.
      Though usually great,
      I do have to state
I'm embarrassed when peanuts are passed."

LAUGH   A nurse once replied, with a laugh,
"You nerd!" to a doc on the staff
      Who'd proposed, with a whine,
      "If you don't sixty-nine,
How 'bout thirty-four and a half?"

LAVERNE   There was a young bride named Laverne,
Who found she'd a great deal to learn.
      The man she had wed
      Took young boys into bed,
And she didn't know which way to turn.

LAY

There was a young temptress who lay
With her legs wide apart in the hay.
　　Then calling a ploughman,
　　She said, "Do it now, man!
Don't wait 'til your hair has turned gray."

LEA

All the streams that water the lea
Are quite pestilential with pee.
　　But the gallons of sperm
　　Spread nary a germ;
In rubbers they float to the sea.

LEAR

There was an old farmer named Lear
Who possessed a fine cow that gave beer.
　　Budweiser and Schlitz
　　Could be tapped from her tits,
And pretzels came out of the rear.

LEE

A Quaker bartender named Lee
Shunned fights assiduously,
　　But got up his ire
　　At religious inquire,
And quietly murmured, "Fuck thee!"

LEE

I dined with the Duchess of Lee,
Who asked, "Do you fart when you pee?"
　　I replied, with some wit,
　　"Do you belch when you shit?"
And felt it was one-up to me.

LEEDS

There once was a farmer of Leeds
Who swallowed a packet of seeds.
　　When the first week was over,
　　He sprouted in clover,
And couldn't sit down for the weeds.

LEEDS   There once was a lecher of Leeds
Who did up his privates in tweeds,
   With a zipper installed,
   To keep them close-hauled,
Or released for his amorous needs.

LEEMAN   A curvaceous young lady named Leeman
Refused naval dates with much screamin'.
   It was not that the army
   Was any more charmy,
But the gal was allergic to seamen.

LEIGH   There was a young plumber of Leigh,
Who was plumbing a gal by the sea.
   She said, "Stop your plumbing,
   There's somebody coming."
Said the plumber, still plumbing, "It's me!"

LEO

A cowboy, by birthright a Leo,
Once met a young woman in Rio.
    A full night and day
    They spent in the hay,
And now the poor cowboy can't pee-o.

LEON

At Mills, a professor named Leon
Taught heresies most Manichean.
    Quoth the girls, "Though it's pleasant,
    Let's disdain this crude peasant;
Or, as Mexicans say, 'Peon Leon!'"

LESSING

There was a young woman named Lessing,
Whose cock-eating ways were distressing.
    She would insert the head,
    'Twixt two slices of bread,
And munch it without even dressing.

LEVINE

A seamstress named Bertha Levine
Caught her boob in her sewing machine.
    She saw, with distress,
    That stitched on her breast
Was "God Bless Our Home," done in green.

LIFE

Joseph led a real gourmet's life
(Though he always ate pulse with his knife).
    When the cook cried out, "Sir!
    Try this great *pot au feu*,"
Old Joseph tried Potiphar's wife.

LILIOM

To her gardener a lady named Liliom
Said, "Billy, plant roses and trillium."
    Then she started to fool
    With the gardener's tool,
And wound up in a bed of sweet William.

LIMBO   As he struggled to heaven from limbo,
Dante murmured to Beatrice, his bimbo,
  "Sure, you want to scrimmage,
  But think of my image;
Don't just lie there, vagina akimbo!"

LIMOUSINE   An astronomer's swift limousine
Went through a red light in Racine.
  He was going so fast
  That the light that he passed,
Through Doppler effect, showed as green.

LIONHEART   King Richard, a.k.a. Lionheart,
Had bedded a sixpenny tart.
  The girl saw great things,
  For this king among kings,
And was glad to be doing her part.

LISZT   The piano composer named Liszt
Learned to play one-handed as he pissed;
   As he grew older,
   His style grew bolder,
And in concert he jerked off with his fist.

LOCH NESS   There was a young man from Loch Ness,
Whose sexual life was a mess,
   'Til the beast in the Loch
   Bit the head off his cock—
Which solved all his problems, I guess!

LOCKE   A gay prison chaplain named Locke
With a weakness for hard convict cock
   For his assholy ways
   In his Alcatraz days
Was nicknamed "the piece of the Rock."

LODGE

A cautious young fellow named Lodge
Had lap belts installed in his Dodge.
>   When his date was strapped in,
>   He committed a sin,
Without even leaving the g'rage.

LOLITA

A sultry young nymphet, Lolita,
Was expert at eating a peter.
>   She demurely would say,
>   "I shall chew it all day;
I'm a slow but fastidious eater."

LOOK

Abou asked, as he sneaked a quick look,
"What you writin' in that big gold book?"
>   The angel screamed, "Ben!
>   You ask once again,
And I'll take your name off the list, schnook."

LOONT

A Lancashire 'ore named Loont
'Ad a clevah promotional stoont.
    When the hayer was so foul
    You coont see at oul,
She burned a red flayer in her coont.

LORETTA

A lonely old maid named Loretta
Sent herself an anonymous letter,
    Quoting Ellis on sex,
    And *Oedipus Rex,*
She exclaimed, "I already feel better!"

LOU

There once was a sperm cell named Lou,
Who dreamed that an egg tryst was due.
    But his dream was a dud,
    For his swinging host's pud
Launched him into the mouth of one Sue.

LOUTH

There was a young maiden of Louth,
Who returned from a trip in the South.
  Her father said, "Nelly,
  There's more in your belly
Than ever went in by your mouth!"

LOWE

A daredevil skater named Lowe
Leaps barrels arranged in the snow,
  But is proudest of doing
  Some incredible screwing—
Once he jumped thirteen girls in a row!

LUGGER

There was a young mate of a lugger,
Who took out a girl, just to hug her.
  "I've my monthlies," she said,
  "And a cold in my head,
But my bowels are all right. Do you bugger?"

LUNDY　　There was an old parson of Lundy,
Fell asleep in the vestry on Sunday.
　　He awoke with a scream,
　　"What! Another wet dream?
That comes of not frigging since Monday!"

LUPESCU　　The beautiful Madame Lupescu
Once came to Rumania's rescue.
　　It's a very fine thing
　　To be under a king;
Is democracy better? I esk you.

LYME　　There was a young fellow from Lyme
Who married three wives at one time.
　　When asked, "Why the third?"
　　He replied, "One's absurd,
And bigamy, sir, is a crime!"

LYNN

There was a young fellow from Lynn,
Whose cock was the size of a pin.
    Said his girl, with a laugh,
    As she fondled his staff,
"Well, *this* won't be much of a sin."

MACFOOSHAN

There once was a Scot named MacFooshan
Whose tool had an odd convolution;
    Whenever he'd pass
    A comely young lass,
The tilt of his kilt caused confusion.

MADDER

As Titian was mixing rose madder,
His model ascended the ladder.
    Her position to Titian
    Suggested coition,
So he mounted the ladder and had her.

MADRAS   There was a young maid from Madras
Who had a magnificent ass,
>   Not rounded and pink,
>   As you probably think—
It was gray, had long ears, and ate grass.

MADRAS   There was a young man of Madras
Who was masturbating in the grass,
>   When a *cobra de capello*
>   Said, "Hello, young fellow!"
And bit a piece out of his ass.

MADRID   An unfortunate man from Madrid
Had only superego and id.
>   So whether he screwed
>   Or entirely eschewed,
He suffered, whatever he did.

MADRID

There was a young girl from Madrid,
Who said she had never been rid.
    Then came an Italian,
    Hung like a stallion,
Who said that he would…and he did.

MAGUIRE

A gay man by the name of Maguire
Hung a sign out ASSHOLE FOR HIRE:
    YOU CAN BUY BY THE PIECE
    OR ON QUARTERLY LEASE;
FOR CLERICAL RATES, PLEASE ENQUIRE.

MAHLER

A German musician named Mahler
Had his balls insured for a dollar.
    One ball was petite,
    Like a wee grain of wheat,
The other, remarkably, smaller.

MAHOUT

There was an old Hindu mahout
Who said, "What's all this blithering about?
    Why, I have shot spunk
    Up an elephant's trunk."
Cries of "Shame!" "Kick his ass!" "Throw him out!"

MAID

Joan of Arc was renowned as a maid;
That means she had never been laid.
    She wore iron britches
    With stainless steel stitches,
Which is why she was never afraid.

MAINE

There was a young woman from Maine
Whose face was exceedingly plain,
    But her mons had a pucker
    Such that men liked to fuck her
Again and again and again.

MALE
Mercurians, female and male,
Whenever they tear off some tail,
　　Do all of their lovin'
　　Inside of an oven—
They think of us Earthlings as frail.

MALOFF
Said a famous French chef, Jean Maloff,
"Though my omelets are tiny and tough,
　　Let the customers beg
　　For more than one egg—
For a Frenchman, one egg is *un oeuf!*"

MALOTTE
Said a zookeeper's wife named Malotte,
As she stuffed some live ants up her twat,
　　"Of all sexual sensations,
　　The eccentric gyrations
Of an anteater's tongue tops the lot."

MAN   Moses was a constipated man.
For guidance to Mt. Sinai he ran.
From a bush, the Lord hissed,
"I'll give you an assist—
Here're two tablets; they're called Serutan."

MANILA   A Good Humor man from Manila
Stuck a freezer inside a gorilla
Which, when fed the right food
And swirlingly screwed,
Crapped chocolate, orange ice, and vanilla.

MARGE   There was a young maiden named Marge,
Who swam in the nude from a barge.
'Til a man in a boat
Disappeared down her throat,
An organ admittedly large.

MARINE
There was a young Royal Marine
Whose musical ear was obscene.
    He said, "Isn't it odd,
    But I never know 'God
Save the Weasel' from 'Pop Goes the Queen.'"

MARINE
To his girl said a Cornish marine,
"You've the knobbiest coastline I've seen.
    To put into port
    Would be jolly good sport,
If the rest of the fleet hadn't been."

MARKS
If Leo your own birthday marks,
You'll have sex until sixty, when starts
    An interest in stamps,
    Boy Scouts, and their camps,
And fondling nude statues in parks.

MARRS "I'll stand up for my rights," yelled Miss Marrs,
But all she could show were some scars.
For the males, as one, rose
And resorted to blows,
When she crashed homosexual bars.

MARTHA There was a young lady named Martha;
When the girls went far, she went fartha.
The affairs were good fun,
The result was a son,
Named Lincoln Dean "Douglas" McArtha.

MASSES Young Joe is just one of the masses
Of guys quite adept with the lasses.
He remarked with some fright,
As he kissed her goodnight,
"Spread your legs, dear, you're breaking my glasses!"

MATE

In Oz land the Tin Woodsman's mate
Sighed sadly, "It sure would be great
    If you made it a point
    To put oil on your joint,
Since your screws have been rusty of late."

MATHER

Heart transplant patient Tom Mather
Worked himself into a lather.
    Said he, "The idea's good,
    But, God, if I could
Get a new prostate gland, I'd much rather."

MAY

An airborne executive, May,
Achieved new heights this fine day;
    She screwed without quittin'
    From New York to Britain—
It's clear she has come a long way.

MAYS A hungry young linguist named Mays
Played with a fruit salad for days.
    "To hell with a cherry,
    I seek a red berry,
If permitted to coign a *fraise*."

MCBRIDE There was a young man named McBride,
Who fell in a privy and died.
    The next day his brother
    Fell into another,
And now they're interred, side by side.

MCCOMB There was an old maid named McComb
Who liked her men tall and handsome.
    (She could also make do
    With a finger or two,
Or the end of her calloused old thumb.)

MCGEE

"How, I wonder," said Sarah McGee,
"Why my lover's lost interest in me;
    Is it that I can't dance,
    Or the lock on my pants
For which I won't give him the key?"

MCGILL

The dong of a dean of McGill
Was adorned with a porcupine quill.
    "It looks odd," he agreed,
    "But the thing's guaranteed
To provide an additional thrill."

MCGILL

While they ate at the diner, McGill
Planned his conquest with cunning and skill:
    He unzipped, wrapped a ten
    'Round his manhood, and then
Told his date she'd be stuck with the bill!

MCGUFF "Great God!" wailed Peter McGuff,
"What the hell is all of this stuff!
    She twiddles my prick,
    Gets it stiff as a stick,
Then denies me the use of her muff!"

MCGURK There was a young man named McGurk
Who dozed off one night after work.
    He had a wet dream,
    And awoke with a scream,
Just in time to give it a jerk.

MCHUGH There was a young man named McHugh,
Whose ideas were exciting and new,
    But an ancient relation
    Gave disapprobation
To McHugh spelling *fuq* (with a *q*).

MCKESSON A curious old maid named McKesson
Walked in while a man was undressin'.
　　　His face turned beet-red,
　　　But she smiled and then said,
"I'm too ancient to find this distressin'."

MCMITCHIN There was a young girl named McMitchin
Who was scratching herself in the kitchen.
　　　Her mother said, "Rose,
　　　It's crabs, I suppose?"
Rose said, "Yes, and, by Jesus, they're itchin'!"

MCNAIR A balding young man named McNair
Patched his pate with the snatch of a bear.
　　　Said he, "A shampoo
　　　Is as good as a screw,
And I come when I'm combing my hair."

MCNAMITER There was a young man named McNamiter
With a tool of prodigious diameter.
    But it wasn't the size
    Gave the girls a surprise,
But his rhythm: iambic pentameter.

MCNARY Said his virginal bride to McNary,
"I've saved myself just for you, Harry."
    But to his chagrin,
    When he screwed his way in,
He found there were seeds in her cherry.

MCNEFF The cross-eyed old painter, McNeff,
Was color-blind, palsied, and deaf.
    When he asked to be touted,
    The critics all shouted,
"This is art with a capital *F*!"

MCPHERSON A happy old hag named McPherson
Was really the *busiest* person;
    Spent her days, it's a fact,
    In the sexual act,
And all of her nights in rehearsing.

MCQUEEN A daring gay man named McQueen
Would keep watch in a public latrine,
    And when his bold gaze
    Caused a member to raise
Why, then he'd start making the seen.

MCSIDNEY The great Glasgow surgeon, McSidney,
Was convinced if he transferred a kidney
    From a whale to a conger
    It would piss a lot longer.
He could not have been wronger: it didna.

MCSWILL

A hot Dean of Women, McSwill,
Took the contraceptivity pill.
        For one lovely semester
        Any man could molest her—
Her need for resistance was nil.

MCWHINNERS

A divine by the name of McWhinners
Held classes each evening for sinners.
        They were sectioned and graded
        So the very degraded
Would not be held back by beginners.

MCWILDE

Said a man-hater, Willa McWilde,
"Godammit, I find I'm with child.
        But the heart of the bother
        Was telling the father;
The son-of-a-bitch only smiled!"

MEMBER   Being cursed with a very long member,
My friend Long Dong Dunn must remember
  To open his fly
  On the Fourth of July,
In order to pee by September.

MEN   Brave Daniel was a man among men,
And for football he had a great yen.
  He became so adroit
  He was tapped by Detroit,
And was cast into the Lions' den.

MEN   Pass not this lonely grave by, men.
Pass not without a deep sigh, men.
  For here lies Jane Jorgans,
  With each of her organs,
Including, alas, her own hymen.

MENTION
A young man, whose name we won't mention,
Had a transplant to lower his tension.
    At the beat of his heart,
    He'd let out a fart,
And his penis would snap to attention.

MERTON
There was a young fellow from Merton
Who went out with only his shirt on,
    From which did peep shyly
    His *membrum virile,*
For people to animadvert on.

METUCHEN
A meticulous man from Metuchen
Had a small flea upon his escutcheon.
    When asked, "Why the flea?"
    He replied, "Well, you see,
There wasn't much room to put much in."

MILNOCKET　A curious lad in Milnocket
Went to bed with a solid-fuel rocket.
　　　As he tossed in his sleep,
　　　He ignited the heap;
Now he's worn by his girl in a locket.

MISS　There was an aesthetic young miss
Who thought it the apex of bliss
　　　To jazz herself silly
　　　With the bud of a lily,
Then go to the garden and piss.

MISS WEST　In sex edutcation, Miss West
Said, "Johnny, your work has regressed!
　　　But since learning's a tool,
　　　If you stay after school,
I will help you bone up for the test."

MISSION

A certain young person of Mission,
In a sadly befuddled condition,
Confused picture and song
And declared to a throng
That *The Lady in Red* was by Titian.

MISSION

The Venusians, out on a mission,
Found Earth in a puzzling condition.
They could understand part
Of our laws and our art,
But got stuck in the fifteenth position.

MITHRIDATES

Of that terrible King, Mithridates,
His subjects along the Euphrates
Used to say with great scorn,
"He's not of woman born,
But extruded from fatherly nates."

MOHICAN   I once knew a crazy Mohican
Who got all his jollies from peekin'.
　　　He liked to watch bears
　　　Carry on their affairs,
And the rooster seducing the chicken.

**MOLL
FLANDERS**   Consider the life of Moll Flanders,
Which was spent among harlots and panders,
　　　'Til that worn-out old bitch
　　　Became suddenly rich
On a stock-market tip from Ann Landers.

MONEY   A man who came into some money
Decided to marry a Bunny,
　　　But the thought of the ears
　　　And the tails of the dears
Made him skip it as being too funny.

MONIQUE   When pinched on the fanny, Monique
                Was overcome by a feeling of pique;
                    Exclaiming with verve
                    To her pincher, "Some nerve!"
                He replied, "And in your case, some cheek!"

MONTROSE   There was an old whore in Montrose
                Who'd go off any time that she chose.
                    She could do it, they say,
                    Ninety-nine times a day,
                And if that is no record, it's close.

MONTROSE   There was a young lad from Montrose
                Who could diddle himself with his toes.
                    It was such a great treat,
                    He fell in love with his feet,
                And christened them Myrtle and Rose.

MORAVIA

There was a young girl of Moravia
Whose beauty would surely enslave ya,
  And her double-knee action
  Lent greater attraction
To her happy amoral behavior.

MORGAN

A surgeon named Timothy Morgan
Was a whiz at transplanting an organ.
  For twenty-five grand,
  He'd install one goat gland,
One prick, and two balls...quite a bargain!

MOSE

They stitched a new gland into Mose,
But some untoward symptoms arose;
    When he fingered a quiff,
    It made his ears stiff,
And then he would come through the nose.

Mose's wife cried, "I'd not give two pins
For our chances to breed kiths or kins!"
    But Mose sank to his knees
    And managed to sneeze,
And now he's the father of twins.

MOSES

A religious young miner named Moses
Contracted pneumonoultramicroscopicsilico-
    volcanoconiosis.
    This, plus the schism
    Between Mary Baker Eddy and antidis-
    establishmentarianism,
Made him feel supercalifragilisticexpialidocious.

MOUNTAIN

There was an old man of the mountain,
Who jerked himself off in a fountain.
　　Fifteen times had he spent,
　　Still he wasn't content—
He simply got tired of counting.

MRS. COFFIN

Her daughter, thought worried Mrs. Coffin,
Had morals the city might soften.
　　So she phoned and asked, "Lynne,
　　Are you living in sin?"
Lynne said, "No, but I visit there often."

MULLER

"Are the tarts," they asked astronaut Muller,
"On Uranus more lively…or duller?"
　　He replied, "They're obscene!
　　Their vaginas are green!
They are whores of a different color."

MUNN Said the bank teller, "Sorry, Miss Munn,
But as an escort you've just been undone
    By a client named Beck
    Who's canceled his check
On the grounds of inadequate fun."

MYRTLE There was a young lady named Myrtle
Who had an affair with a turtle.
    She bore crabs, so they say,
    In nine months and a day,
Which proves that the turtle was fertile.

MYRTLE This cute English lassie named Myrtle
Was so fecund and fruitful and fertile,
    She was got with a child
    By Sir Christopher Wilde
Through a crack in her chastity girdle.

MYSTERY

The *Iliad's* really no mystery,
Though details are blustery and blistery.
　　It's a long story tellin'
　　Of the search for Queen Helen,
And the prize horse's ass in all history.

NAME

On Eros, despite its fair name,
The sexes are one and the same.
　　If amusing oneself
　　By abusing oneself
Leads to pregnancy, isn't life tame?

NANCI

A comely masseuse known as Nanci
Was struck by a lewd passing fancy
　　She lubed up with hot oil,
　　Brought herself to a boil,
All while wearing her underpantsy
In a flat just north of Delancey.

NANTUCKET She exulted while touring Nantucket,
"I've a cherry and no one can pluck it!"
        Said her guide, with a smile,
        "I was raised on this isle.
You've a virginal clam? I could shuck it."

NATION Though each brave of the Cherokee nation
May discover some baroque elation
        In beating his prick
        With a hickory stick,
I am sure it's a rare recreation.

NATION Though the virile young priests of the nation
Waited breathless throughout its gestation,
        The bull of Pope John Paul
        Offered nothing at all,
Save prolonged and restrained celibation.

NATION
There are female police in our nation
Who play house with the guys at the station;
    Which is saying, of course,
    That they screw with the force—
After all, folks, the term's *copulation*.

NATTICK
There was a young lady from Nattick
Whose sex life was very erratic.
    She dodged every feller,
    From third floor to cellar,
But slept with them all in the attic.

NEATER
There never was anything neater
Than the bishop of Chichester's peter.
    In the heat of a clinch
    It would stretch from an inch
To just a bit short of a meter.

NEFARIOUS

There's a priest who's classed as nefarious,
Since his shocking perversions are various:
    He will bugger a lass
    With a dildo (at mass!)
While exulting, "My pleasure's vicarious!"

NEFERTITI

The vagina of Queen Nefertiti
Was known to be quite itty-bitty,
    'Til she got, with great trammel,
    The old twat of a camel,
And then she could screw the whole city.

NELL

There was a young lady named Nell
Whose panties were holey as hell.
    She complained, "When I fart,
    My shoes fall apart,
And my ankles occasionally swell."

NERO

Consider the Emperor Nero
(Of many lewd tales he's the hero);
    Though he scraped the fiddle,
    He just couldn't diddle,
And his real batting average was zero.

NE'S'RY

Said a jealous old maid, "Men aren't ne's'ry,
And a penis is just an access'ry.
    For freedom from fear
    And a thrill in the rear,
I'll stick to my old rubber pess'ry!"

NEW YORK

Said a verbal young man from New York,
To his girl while inserting his dork:
    "I prefer you askew,
    Since we chat as we screw,
So I'd welcome some feminine torque."

NICE

A fisherman in medieval Nice
Was instantly ordered to cease
    His naughty deception
    When, during inspection,
They found a real cod in his piece.

NIECE

Have you heard of Tolstoi's hot niece,
A delectable morsel named Lys?
    Need I say more?
    She was the war,
And Tolstoi the one seeking peace.

NORWAY

There was a young lady of Norway
Who hung by her heels in a doorway.
    She said to her beau,
    "Just look at me, Joe.
I think I've discovered one more way."

NORWAY

There was a young man from Norway,
Who was jazzing his girl in a sleigh,
    But the weather was frigid
    And froze his balls rigid,
So all he could shoot was frappé.

NOTRE DAME

A bailardus of old Notre Dame
Was proud of his scholarly fame,
    'Til he got him a piece
    From the canon's sweet niece,
And lost both his stones for the same.

OAK

A speedy young jeweler named Oak
Fixed clocks that were damaged and broke.
    He opened the face
    And in a short space
He changed hands without missing a stroke.

OBSCENE   Old King Louis and court were obscene;
They would screw day and night...and the queen!
    But they made one great error;
    They hung round for the Terror—
Guillotine! Guillotine! Guillotine!

OEDIPUS REX   The play about Oedipus Rex
Has a plot that is very complex.
    He clobbered his pa,
    And then screwed his ma,
While the Chorus sang songs about sex.

OFFER
*(apologies
to William
Faulkner)*
    Some writers have romance to offer;
Black humor is all I can proffer.
    Let's all laugh at the Snopes,
    Those hilarious dopes
From Yok-Yok-Yok-Yoknapatawpha.

OKLAHOMA   A woman from West Oklahoma
Always came when she heard "La Paloma."
> While in Mexico City—
> Ah! More is the pity—
The woman stayed in a deep coma.

OSTEND   There was a young girl of Ostend
Who her maidenhead tried to defend,
> But a *chasseur d'Afrique*
> Inserted his *prique*
And showed that young girl how to spend!

OSTEND   There was a young man of Ostend
Whose wife caught him fucking her friend.
> "It's no use, my duck,
> Interrupting our fuck,
For I'm damned if I'll draw 'til I spend!"

PARENTIS　　Said two farm boys, *in loco parentis,*
"This new lingo is gonna dement us—
　　　Like *ordure* and *offal,*
　　　They sound just plain awful.
It is driving us *non compost mentis.*"

PARMA　　There was a young warrior of Parma
Who got into bed with a charmer.
　　　She—naturally—nude,
　　　Said, "Don't think me rude,
But I *do* wish you'd take off your armor."

PARMIMAHANDA　　A yogi named Parmimahanda
Thought love with a cobra was danda,
　　　'Til a flick of the fang
　　　In the shank of the yang
Left him dead upon the veranda.

PAUL There once was a flasher named Paul
Who stationed himself in a mall.
    He unzipped as he bowed
    To the curious crowd
Then extended his welcome to all.

PEASE A zoology major named Pease
Begged her prof for an A and some B's.
    He toyed with her C,
    Then showed her his D;
She was finally bedded with E's.

PECK There was a young sailor named Peck
Who kept his passions in check
    By dwelling on rumors
    Of penile tumors,
And beating his meat below deck.

PENZANCE

There was a young man of Penzance
Who rogered his three maiden aunts.
Though them he defiled,
He ne'er got them with child,
Through using the letters of France.

PERSIANS

A remarkable race are the Persians;
They have such peculiar diversions.
They screw the whole day
In the regular way,
And at night they get up to perversions.

PERU

A rabbi who lived in Peru
Was vainly attempting to screw.
His wife said, "Oy veh!
If you keep on this way,
The Messiah will come before you."

PERU Said a classicist down in Peru
"When in love you can best follow through
    And show your devotion
    With the helical motion
Of the great Archimedean screw."

PERU There was a young girl from Peru
Who regretted her lovers were few,
    So she walked from her door,
    With a fig leaf, no more—
And now she's in bed with the flu!

PERU There was a young man of Peru
Who was hard up for something to do,
    So he took out his carrot
    And buggered his parrot,
And sent the results to the zoo.

PET

The Venusians do not kiss or pet
Or work themselves into a sweat
    About sex; they get wed,
    Then all feeling goes dead—
Just how alien can you get?

PETE

A flexible fellow named Pete,
Who took a flashlight 'neath the sheet,
    Was asked to tell why.
    This was his reply:
"I really must watch what I eat."

PHIDIAS

There once was a sculptor named Phidias
Whose influence on art was invidious.
    On a statue of Venus
    He carved a huge penis,
Thus shocking the ultra-fastidious.

PHIL

A brazen young fellow named Phil
Agreed to test out a new pill;
    His kidneys eroded,
    Both buttocks exploded,
And his penis was found in Brazil.

PHIPPS

At death's door lay Alicia Phipps.
No man had yet mounted her hips.
    As sadly she waited,
    One intern palpitated;
She died with a smile on her lips.

PICTURE PALACES

The girls who frequent picture palaces
Set no store by psychoanalysis,
    And though Dr. Freud
    Is greatly annoyed,
They cling to their old-fashioned phalluses.

PISCES

A lesbian born under Pisces
Has dildos of several sizes.
    The one made of quartz
    She keeps in her shorts,
So she can goose herself in the thighses.

PLAINER

"Each year," said a Wells girl, "it's plainer;
Cramming's vain, class attendance is vainer.
    To get A in Phys Ed
    I just worked out in bed
With the wrestling coach and the trainer."

PLASTERED

The bachelor girl who gets plastered
And fears she'll be screwed by some bastard
    Should get her physician
    To make an incision,
And be doctored before she is mastered.

POITAN
The College of Arms of Poitan
Ennobled a lowly-born man
　　Because (we are told)
　　He handed out gold
And slave girls who danced with a fan.

POLYP
An irate young husband named Polyp
Lashed out with a terrible wallop
　　At an overnight guest
　　Who dared to suggest
That his wife was an ord'nary trollop.

POOLE
An English conductor named Poole
Conducted Brahms's First with his tool.
　　Such ambidexterity,
　　Grace, and celerity!
(The critical comment was "cool.")

POPSICLES   A divorcée, cold as popsicles,
Waived all her ex-husband's nickels.
    She transplanted, instead,
    To each side of her head,
Two earrings carved from his testicles.

PORT SAID   There was a young man of Port Said
Whose penis grew tattered and frayed,
    Thus earning him taunts
    From his well-meaning aunts,
And complaints from the women he laid.

PRATT   A sharp old musician named Pratt
Had a staff that was *breve* but fat.
    Though he owned a *château*,
    He felt *obbligato*
To bugger his wife in A-flat.

PRETTY She wasn't what one would call pretty,
And other girls offered her pity,
    So nobody guessed
    That her Wassermann test
Involved half the men in the city.

PROCTOR A patient of young Doctor Proctor
Didn't mind when he swiftly unfroctor.
    Nor did his technique
    Give her reason to squique,
Until *after* she found he'd upknocktor.

PROPORTIONS Cecilia of ample proportion
Took all contraceptive precautions,
    But thin little Ermintrude
    Let a small sperm intrude.
Do you know a good man for abortions?

PRU

A coquettish young woman named Pru
Thought her peekaboo blouse was a coup,
　　But returned to the shop
　　And declared it a flop,
For the fellows would peek but not screw!

PRUITT

A virginal fellow named Pruitt
Once asked to be shown how to do it;
　　But it soon became clear
　　That his mentor was queer—
And the upshot was, young Pruitt blew it.

PURDUE

Said a passionate girl from Purdue
To her German professor, Karl Drew,
　　"You think reading Nietzsche
　　Is perfectly peachy,
But, frankly, I'd much rather screw."

PURDUE

There was a young man from Purdue,
Who was only just learning to screw,
But he hadn't the knack,
He'd lean too far back—
The right church, so to speak, but wrong pew.

RACINE

There was a young man from Racine
Who invented a fucking machine.
Concave or convex,
It would fit either sex,
And was perfectly simple to clean.

RACINE

There was a young man of Racine
Who was weaned at the age of sixteen.
He said, "I'll admit
There's no milk in the tit,
But think of the fun it has been!"

RAINES
An ardent campaigner named Raines
When parading for feminine gains,
    Was arrested at once
    For engaging in stunts
That left several permanent stains.

RALEIGH
A well-bred young miss from old Raleigh
Met a man from New York on the traleigh.
    When she said to the guy,
    "Y'all come, don't be shy,"
He gave her a valeigh, by galeigh!

RANGOON
An ardent Scots lass in Rangoon
Went down on a Burmese quadroon.
    While the rising wind rasped
    Round the temple, she gasped,
"What a night for a blow! Come, mon—soon!"

RANGOON
There was a young man from Rangoon,
Whose farts could be heard to the moon.
    When you wouldn't expect 'em,
    They would rush from his rectum,
Like the roar of a double bassoon.

RANSOM
There was a young lady named Ransom,
Who was rogered three times in a hansom.
    When she cried out for more,
    A voice from the floor
Said, "My name is Simpson...not Samson."

RANTED A well-known mesmerist ranted
That a spell could not be recanted.
   "Could it be?" was the question,
   "Post-hypnotic suggestion
Is a thought that's forever trance-planted?"

RAPE The duchess of Whiteside cried, "Rape!"
When she found in her bedroom an ape.
   The ape said, "You ass!
   Go look in the glass,"
And left by the fire escape.

RAWLS There was a young fellow named Rawls,
Who slipped from the dome of St. Paul's,
   But the angels of grace
   Sped thither apace,
And lowered him down by his balls.

READING

There was a young fellow of Reading
Who grew so aroused at his wedding;
    At the sight of his bride,
    When he got her inside,
He creamed all over the bedding.

REILLY

There once was a widow named Reilly,
Who esteemed her late husband most highly,
    And, in spite of the scandal,
    Her umbrella handle
Was made of his *membrum virile*.

REMEMBERS

Says an old maid, when she remembers,
"Now my days are quite clearly Septembers.
    All my fires have burned low,
    I'll admit that it's so,
But you still might have fun in the embers."

RENOWN

There was a young girl of renown
Who'd stroll through the streets in her gown;
    Constructed of leather,
    And resistant to weather,
It forced her to screw standing up.

REX

A young Scottish soldier named Rex
Abstains with great zeal from all sex.
    He is such a Spartan
    Because of his tartan;
He suffers from a kilt complex.

RHEIMS

A crafty old bugler of Rheims
Would feast upon coconut creams,
    And fart a toccata
    Or a Mozart sonata
On seventeenth-century themes.

RHEIMS   There was a young fellow of Rheims
Who was terribly plagued with wet dreams.
He saved up a half-dozen
And sent them to his cousin,
Who ate them and thought they were creams.

RIO   A young violinist from Rio
Was seducing a woman named Cleo.
As she took down her panties,
She said, "No *andantes;*
I want this *allegro con brio*."

RITZ   There was a young man from the Ritz
Who planted an acre of tits.
They came up in the fall,
Red nipples and all,
And he leisurely chewed them to bits.

ROBIN HOOD

A bandit was bold Robin Hood,
Whose motives were misunderstood.
  He took tons of riches
  From rich sons-of-bitches,
And reviled them while pulling his pud.

RODGERS

There once was a young girl named Rodgers,
An apprentice who played with the lodgers,
  And two who were able
  Slipped under the table,
To the horror of several old codgers.

ROLLED RUG

I breathe as though wrapped in a rolled rug;
My nose is stopped up like an old jug.
  I must stop my ravin';
  It's dreamland I'm cravin'
But how can I sleep with this cold bug?

ROLLO

When a hillbilly lover named Rollo
Asked a girl as they sparked in the hollow,
    "Did you know that my dong
    Measures nine inches long?"
She replied, "That's a hard one to swallow!"

ROOS

A miscegenator named Roos
Spent a week in Rangoon on the loose
    After trying all races
    On an impartial basis,
His favorite hue remains puce.

ROWELL

A certain young lady named Rowell
Had a musical vent to her bowel.
    With a good plate of beans
    Tucked under her jeans,
She could play "To a Wild Rose" by MacDowell.

RUMMING

Are you looking for wenching and rumming?
In India, everyone's humming:
    With a Hindu gal, sex
    Is so gaily complex,
You won't know if you're going or coming.

RUSSELL

To probe Miss Lillian Russell,
Dr. Long thrust a pin through her bustle.
    He got a sprained wrist,
    And a mouthful of fist,
For the bustle turned out to be muscle.

SAGITTARIUS

The men of the sign Sagittarius
Have customs obscene and barbarious.
    They sow their wild oats
    With girls, boys, and goats,
In postures ingenious and various.

ST. BEES There was an old man of St. Bees,
Who was stung in the arm by a wasp.
  When asked, "Does it hurt?"
  He replied, "No, it doesn't.
I'm so glad it wasn't a hornet."

ST. BEES There was a young *man* of St. Bees,
Who said to his girl, "If you please,
  While playing with this,
  It would give me great bliss,
If you'd pay some attention to these."

There was a young *girl* of St. Bees,
Who said to her beau, "If you please,
  While playing with this,
  It would give me great bliss,
If you'd pay some attention to these."

ST. JOHN'S

There was a young lad of St. John's
Who wanted to bugger the swans,
    But the loyal hall porter
    Said, "No! Take my daughter.
Them birds is reserved for the dons!"

ST. JUST

The prior of Dunstan St. Just
Overcome with feelings of lust,
    Satisfied his strange urgin'
    With a bust of the Virgin
And a water pump covered in rust.

ST. PAUL

An original miss from St. Paul
Wore a newspaper dress to a ball,
    But the dress caught on fire,
    And burnt her entire,
Front page, sports section, and all.

ST. PAUL   There was an old maid from St. Paul
Who went to the birth-control hall.
     She was loaded with pessaries
     And other accessories,
But nobody asked her to ball.

ST. PAUL   There was a young man from St. Paul
Who went to a fancy dress ball.
     He went off in his pants
     In the midst of a dance,
And had to go home in a shawl.

ST. PAUL'S   Said the venerable dean of St. Paul's,
"Concerning them cracks in the walls,
     Do you think it would do
     If we filled them with glue?"
The bishop of London said, "Balls!"

ST. PAUL'S

There was a young man of St. Paul's,
Who dreamt of Niagara Falls.
> When he woke the next day,
> It was "Anchors Aweigh!"
For his penis, his ass, and his balls.

SAKI

In a scene reminiscent of Saki,
Stumpy Joe saw Dr. Michael de Bakey,
> Then used his transplant
> To deflower his aunt,
And took off for Paris, quite cocky.

SALINAS

Nympho Venus, who hailed from Salinas,
Had a thing for medical penis.
> When her doc gave her shots,
> She contracted the hots—
Curable only with shots intra-Venus.

SALLOW

A lesbian of complexion quite sallow
Said, "Pricks are like wicks without tallow.
    From Paris to China,
    Most men choose vagina—
It's so very much easier to swallow!"

SALLY

There was an equestrienne, Sally,
Who went with her groom up an alley.
    There was naught she could do;
    He was too young to screw.
She muttered, "How Green Was My Valet!"

SAMOA

There was a young girl of Samoa
Who boasted that no man could know her.
    One young fellow tried,
    But she wriggled aside,
And he spilled his spermatozoa.

SANS SOUCI

Said a Frenchman who lived at Sans Souci,
"Superstition? *Mon Dieu! C'est tout fou, si?*
    Why only *ce soir*
    I buggaired *un chat noir;*
To *un homme virile*, poussy is poussy!"

SCARRED

A northerner, ragged and scarred,
Displayed to a wandering bard
    A shield for his back,
    All battered and black,
And remarked it was called his Asgard.

SCHIFF

An arrogant Nazi named Schiff
Broke up with his wife in a tiff.
    Though he did not lack charm,
    She complained that his arm
Was the only thing he could keep stiff.

SCREW
He was known as a wonderful screw,
With his dink in the pink all day through,
    But the fine days of plenty
    Were done after twenty,
When the red in his balls turned to blue.

SCREW
The right to decide when to screw
Is one that we all now pursue.
    But back in the day,
    Girls got no real say
In either how much or with who.

SEA
There was a young lady at sea,
Who complained that it hurt her to pee.
    "Aha!" said the mate,
    "*That* accounts for the state
Of the captain, the boatswain, and me."

SEARS

In the catalog published by Sears,
A layout by Dali appears.
    It depicts a June bride
    With three breasts on each side,
Caressing a penis with ears.

SEATTLE

There was a young man from Seattle,
Whose balls were so small they would rattle
    He tried 'em on chickens,
    Got good as the dickens,
And now he can satisfy cattle.

SEEM

O, Shakespeare's love life, it would seem,
Was something not quite on the beam.
    Too lazy to fuck,
    And not wanting to suck,
He preferred *A Midsummer Night's Dream*.

SERENE

Said Napoleon, emperor serene,
While scouting around for a queen,
    "I'd much rather squeeza
    Maria Louisa,
Than sleep with that bitch Josephine."

SET

There once was a priestess of Set
Whom a shaman pursued on a bet.
    Though she turned to a snake,
    The shaman won the stake,
But it's something he'd rather forget.

SHAFTER

Tim said to his wife, up in Shafter,
"Seems to me there's a man in the rafter."
    She smirked, and then said,
    "Come, get into bed;
I'm saving that fellow for after."

SHALOTT

There was a young maid from Shalott,
Who claimed she was hotter than hot.
    She burnt off the hair
    Of a priest from Adair,
Who said it was worth what he got....
    (She burnt off the balls
    Of a priest from St. Paul's,
Who mournfully said it was not!)

SHAW

Cried a great English writer, "Oh, Shaw!
My testes are small as the Dickens."
    Said his surgeon, "Great Scott!
    Here's a fine pair-o'-Keats';
I'll transplant them and make your Balsworthy!"

SHEBA

There was a young woman named Sheba
Who loved a Teutonic amoeba.
    This primordial jelly
    Would crawl on her belly,
And murmur, "*Ich liebe, ich liebe.*"

SHREW

The tiniest mammal, the shrew,
Is known for the three-second screw.
    He'll repeat it at will,
    On any mole hill,
And his head is all that turns blue.

SIAM

There was a young maiden from Siam,
Who said to her lover, young Khayyam,
    "To seduce me, of course,
    You will have to use force.
Thank goodness you're stronger than I am!"

SIAM
These words spoke the king of Siam,
"For women I don't care a damn,
But a fat-bottomed boy
Is my pride and my joy.
You may call me a bugger. I am!"

SIBERIA
There was a young monk of Siberia,
Whose life grew drearier and drearier,
So he did to a nun
What he shouldn't have done,
And made her a Mother Superior.

SIDNEY
There was an old fellow named Sidney,
Who drank 'til he ruined a kidney.
It shriveled and shrank
As he sat there and drank,
But he had a good time of it, didn't he?

SIN
To the doc said his wife, "It's a sin,
But I don't want a baby again.
    To help save our marriage,
    Take my baby carriage,
But I still want to keep my playpen."

SIOUX
An Indian maiden, a Sioux,
As tempting as fresh honeydioux,
    Liked to show off her knees,
    As she strolled past tepees,
To hear the braves holler, "Wioux, Wioux!"

SIOUX
There once was a sensuous Sioux
Who liked to do nothing but scrioux;
    But she gave no relief
    To the tribe's aged chief,
Until both of his balls had turned blioux.

SIOUX FALLS   A strapping young man from Sioux Falls
Is constantly trampling his balls.
    They hang down so low,
    He has to go slow—
And in icy conditions he crawls.

SITE   "This theater is a state landmark site."
(from a Tourist
Guide Book)   "The box office is just to your right."
    "The first show is at ten."
    "Where's the room for the men?"
"Do you have any seats for tonight?"

SKINNER
There was a young fellow named Skinner
Who took a young lady to dinner.
    They sat down to dine
    At a quarter past nine,
At a quarter past ten it was in her
    (the dinner, not Skinner—
    Skinner was in her before dinner).

There was a young fellow named Tupper
Who took a young lady to supper.
    They sat down to dine
    At a quarter past nine,
At a quarter to ten, it was up her
    (not the supper, not Tupper,
But some son-of-a-bitch named Skinner).

SLOUGH
There was a young maiden of Slough,
Who said that she didn't know how.
    Then a young fellow caught her,
    And jolly well taught her;
She lodges in Pimlico now.

SLOW

Her sidesaddle progress was slow;
No track tout would rate her a pro.
    Said Godiva, "I rode
    While the townspeople *oh*'d—
Not to win or to place, but to show!"

SMALL

The Plutonian male is so small
He lives in the vaginal wall
    Of his mate. Yes, *de trop*,
    But he *likes* it, you know,
And *chacun à son goût*, after all.

SMITH

At the all-women's college called Smith,
A common and recurring myth
    That a masculine member
    Helps students remember
Was found without substance or pith.

SMITH

Said a pretty young student from Smith,
Whose virtue was largely a myth,
"Try hard as I can,
I can't find a man
Whom it's fun to be virtuous with."

SOME

A cabby's wife, brighter than some,
Had a meter installed in her bum,
With a musical chime
To keep track of the time
And allow you to pay as you come.

SONDANT

A tragic young wife, Mrs. Sondant,
Made complaint in an accent despondent.
The courtroom was sultry;
The charge was adult'ry—
Her brother was named co-respondent.

SOO

A heifer from up near the Soo,
When approached by a bull, answered, "Moo."
    Then she took the wrong tack,
    And lay down on her back,
But the bull figured out what to do.

SOUL

Confession is good for the soul:
I admit that I've dreamed of a hole
    That was not round but square,
    And had silky green hair
So thick it was like a mink stole.

SOULING

Said an eager young surgeon from Souling,
"So far, we have only been fooling.
    But soon it won't vex us
    To change both the sexes,
It's simply a case of retooling."

SOUTH FORKS

There's a woman who lives at South Forks
Makes a fetish of old vermouth corks.
    She keeps those labeled *France*
    In the front of her pants,
And *Italy* back round her porks.

SOUTH JOISEY

A railroad hotel in South Joisey
(Near where they switch trains) is quite noisy.
    A guest phoned the clerk
    And yelled, "Hey, you jerk!
When's this damn hotel get to Boise?"

SPAIN

Then up spoke the young king of Spain:
"To fuck and to bugger may be vain.
    But it's not *infra dig*
    On occasion to frig,
And I do it again and again."

SPAIN

There was a young woman of Spain
Who took down her pants on a train.
    A very young porter
    Saw more than he orter,
And asked her to do it again.

SPAIN

There was a young traveler from Spain
Who did it again and again.
    And again and again
    And again and again
And again and again and again.
(She stopped to get onto a plane,
But picked right back up in Bahrain.)

SPECTRA With color enough for twin spectra,
This plane really needs nothing extra.
    As I walk to the back,
    I rejoice I wore black,
For my mourning becomes Electra.

SPITZBERGEN There was a young girl of Spitzbergen
Whose family all thought her a virgin,
    'Til they found her in bed
    With her mons very red
And the head of a kid just emergin'.

STAR
(for Woodrow Wilson) As a beauty, I am not a star;
There are others more handsome by far.
    But my face, I don't mind it,
    For I am behind it;
It's the fellow in front that I jar.

STATE

"Miss Smith," said the dean, "I must state
As a scholar you don't pull much weight.
 Your math is just terrible,
 Your physics unbearable,
Though I'd say your physique is just great."

STATING

A problem that's very worth stating,
Researching, exploring, debating,
 Is if we can tell,
 From our friends with one cell,
Whether splitting's as much fun as mating.

STEAD

For a phallus, Miss Winifred Stead
Used a bar from the foot of her bed,
 But lacking the touch
 Of blacksmiths and such
Kept her ever from forging ahead.

STONE

Said a haughty old lecher named Stone,
Who had but five inches of bone,
    "I feel no deep urgin'
    To consult a surgeon;
A mighty poor thing, but mine own!"

STOP

Junior's sex in my auto must stop
Or my son must locate a new prop.
    It is a convertible,
    And what's disconcertible
Are the high-heel holes thrust through the top.

STRANGE

The formula's secret and strange,
It's cooked on an old-fashioned range,
    And makes use of juices
    Mentioned by Confucius,
Plus hair from a dog with the mange.

STRENSALL

There was a young fellow of Strensall
Whose prick was as sharp as a pencil.
On the night of his wedding,
It went through the bedding
And shattered the bedroom utensil.

STREWED

A bather whose clothing was strewed
By breezes that left her quite nude
Saw a man come along
And, unless I am wrong,
You expected this line to be lewd.

STUTZ

A feminist rebel named Stutz
Is known to have plenty of guts.
When asked what she'd need
To be totally freed,
She said to her questioner, "Nuts!"

STYLITES   On his pillar sat Simon Stylites,
As his balls turned to iron pyrites,
 And the sun's intense heat
 Slowly blackened his meat;
He should not have worn frilly lace nighties.

SUE   An orgasmic young sex star named Sue
Spiced her act up with rare derring-do.
 Her climatic fame spread
 With an ad blitz that read:
"Coming Soon in a Theater Near You!"

SUZIE   The police arrested young Suzie
For being a militant floozie.
 They took off her clothes,
 But no record shows
There was fuzz on top of her coozie.

SWEET BRIAR

"We are ladies here at Sweet Briar,"
The dean told the girls. "We require
    That you peddle your ass,
    If you must, outside class,
And, at all times, in formal attire."

SWOBODA

There was an old man of Swoboda,
Who'd not pay a whore what he owed her,
    So, with great *savoir faire*,
    She climbed up on a chair,
And pissed in his whisky and soda.

TARSUS

There was a young fellow of Tarsus,
Who felt that he needed catharsis.
    To achieve the purge royal,
    He took croton oil,
Discovering, too late, 'twas for horses.

TART   Though a biblical strip-teasing tart,
Salome was a girl with great heart.
    The truth is that instead
    Of John the Baptist's head,
She had asked a more pertinent part.

TASTE   There was a young lady of taste,
Who kept herself virginal, chaste—
    And stoutly defended
    With bear-traps suspended
By filigree chains from her waist.

TAURUS   A man of the natal sign Taurus
Joined up with a folk-singing chorus,
    But he didn't last long,
    For in every song
He croaked like an old brontosaurus.

TEA **W**e invited the duchess to tea.
It was just as I feared it would be;
  Her rumblings abdominal
  Were simply abominable,
And everyone thought it was me!

TED **S**aid a just-wed professor named Ted,
To a redhead right there in his bed,
  "The weather's so snowy,
  And gusty and blowy,
Won't you swallow my pride, dear, instead?"

TEENS

Our most existentialist teens
Are impatient of lectures by deans
    On restraining desires
    And banking the fires
That burn in their skirts and their jeans.

So they go on exerting their wills
And they use neither condoms nor pills.
    The results are most dire;
    They become dam and sire,
And their parents must pick up the bills.

THALIA

There was a Greek sailor from Thalia
Who had several ways to regale ya.
    The best thing about him
    Was the little pink quim
Just above his huge male genitalia.

THARP

A lady musician named Tharp
Got her bust tangled up in her harp.
   When protest arose,
   She was forced to transpose
Bach's G-Minor Suite to C-sharp.

THREE

On Saturn the sexes are three,
A sad state of affairs, you'll agree.
   For performing *con brio*,
   You must have a trio,
And it even takes two just to pee.

THUN

There was a young lady of Thun
Who was screwed by the man in the moon.
   "Well, it has been great fun,"
   She remarked when he'd done,
"But I'm sorry you came quite so soon."

TIBET

There was a young man of Tibet—
And this is the strangest one yet—
    His prick was so long,
    And so pointed and strong,
He could bugger six Greeks *en brochette*.

TIPPLE

A Northampton professor named Tipple
Loved to suckle his young wife's left nipple.
    Though he did it with ardor,
    He could not get it harder,
And he came without even a ripple.

TIT

My ex-girlfriend's easterly tit
Was tough like an old catcher's mitt;
    The other was lighter
    And softer and whiter.
I wonder what happened to it?

TOTTENHAM   There was a young woman of Tottenham
Whose manners—Good Lord!—she'd forgotten 'em.
When she went to the vicar's,
She took off her knickers,
Because, she said, she was hot in 'em.

TOUCAN   A marvelous bird is the toucan
Who when engaged in a screw can
Stand upon his head,
Shove beak in instead;
If you think that's a cinch, see if you can.

TRAFFICKER   In limericks I'm not a trafficker
For my nature is really seraphicker.
My stomach sits queasily,
I blush far too easily,
And I do not collect pornographicker.

TRALEE

There was a young girl of Tralee,
Whose knowledge of French was *"Oui, oui."*
　　When they asked, *"Parlez-vous?"*
　　She replied, "Same to you!"
And was famed for her bright repartee.

TRANSPLANTS

In these days of grafts and transplants,
A guy really takes quite a chance.
　　Are the charms of his toots
　　Really hers to the roots,
Or are they from one of her aunts?

TRASK

Said an ardent bridegroom named Trask,
"I will grant any boon that you ask."
　　Said his bride, "Fuck me, dearie,
　　Until I grow weary."
He died of old age at the task.

TRENT

A Catholic woman named Trent
Refrained from the sex act for Lent.
　　Although she kept feigning
　　She liked the abstaining,
She was eager to come when Lent went.

TRILLING

What with female Marines, Sargeant Trilling,
Finds his life in the Corps more fulfilling.
　　In the daytime, his skill
　　Is in close-order drill,
While at night, it's in close-ardor drilling.

TRING

There was a young lady of Tring
Who sat by the fire to sing.
　　A piece of hot ash
　　Flew right up her ass,
And burnt all the hair off her quim.

TRIPP

A retiring sailor named Tripp
Had a fling upon leaving his ship;
  But he failed to use care
  In a prostitute's lair,
Which is why Tripp has postnaval drip.

TROY

There was a young woman of Troy,
Who invented a new kind of joy.
  She sugared her quim,
  Both outside and in,
And then had it sucked by a boy.

TRY

The Church, after many a try,
Has developed a birth-control buy
  That's in no way mechanical,
  Though goddamned satanical:
On the end of the dong, graft an eye.

TUCKER

There was an inventor named Tucker
Who built a vagina of yucca,
But he waxed quite obscene
When the fractious machine
Got a grip and refused to unpucker.

TUPHET

There was a young lady from Tuphet,
Whose box was so huge none could stuff it.
They transplanted the twidget
Of a really small midget.
Now she's known as Little Miss Muffit.

TUPPS

A broken-down harlot named Tupps
Was heard to confess, in her cups,
"The height of my folly
Was screwing a collie,
But I got a good price for the pups."

TUTOR

A young university tutor
Fed his sexual past to a computer.
    It rebooted his butt
    And zapped his left nut,
And he found himself totally neuter.

TWICKENHAM

There was a young lady of Twickenham,
Who regretted that men had no prick in 'em.
    On her knees, every day
    To God she would pray
To lengthen and strengthen and thicken 'em.

TWO CITIES

The title *A Tale of Two Cities*
Tends to fill me with numerous pities.
    If I'd had the pickin's
    (Instead of Charles Dickens),
I'dve called it *One Tail and Two Titties*.

TYSON There was a young harlot named Tyson
Who fell quite in love with a bison.
    After unholy coition,
    Her snatch's condition
Was never again so enticing.

UNCLOSE The pink buds have refused to unclose,
The aroma's not much of a *chose*.
    Gardening's been luckless
    For Alice B. Toklas,
Still, a rose is a rose is a rose.

UR There was a young fellow of Ur
Whose peter was covered with fur.
    He delighted to stroke it,
    To pat and to poke it,
For the pleasure of hearing it purr.

VENUS There was a young spaceman from Venus
Who had a prodigious penis.
　　　Cried his girlfriend, "Alas!
　　　It just came out my ass,
And there's still fifteen inches between us!"

VERDUN A skinny old maid from Verdun
Wed a short-peckered son-of-a-gun.
　　　'She said, "I don't care
　　　If there isn't much there;
God knows, it is better than none."

VERSAILLES A pretty girl touring Versailles
Remarked, "It's too bad; I could cry.
　　　I've been here ten days
　　　And not gone to the Louvre."
"Never mind," somebody said, "you're
　　　probably dehydrated; just give it time."

VIABLE

Since transplanting has proved to be viable,
And my dong's been less plied than pliable,
    Why not graft, as a ringer,
    My trusty third finger,
Which, these days, is far more reliable?

VICIOUS

Said the Skidmore prof, "I'm not vicious,
But short skirts bring visions lubricious.
    When I look down my class
    At those acres of ass,
I come in my pants. It's pernicious!"

VOTE

My grandmother fought for the vote,
Then my mother bought gin off the boat.
    Today, my dear wife
    Says I've ruined her life,
And my daughter's applying to Choate.

VUNDRUM

A famous zoologist, Vundrum,
Was posed a perplexing conundrum:
    Where to locate what falls
    From an elephant's balls.
And he said, "Vy, it's zimple; look undrum."

WALES

There once was a sailor from Wales,
An expert in pissing in gales.
    He could pee in a jar
    From the top-gallant spar
Without even wetting the sails.

WALL
*(Mene mene
tekel upharsin)*

Read the message that's writ on the wall,
In fiery script ten feet tall,
    And, in case Hebrew
    Is all Greek to you,
I'll translate: It says FUCK YOU ALL.

WALT   A Civil War nurse, by name Walt,
Said, "It really isn't my fault.
  In wartime, it is clear,
  Those we stick in the rear
Are the sick, and the lame, and the halt."

WATERS   Come to Noah's for wine and strong waters,
And for diddling in clean, classy quarters.
  I assure every guest
  That they'll get no rest—
Just ask any one of my daughters.

WAY   To be your own man is the way
To feel like a king every day.
  But don't be your own queen—
  It's not that it's unclean,
But we've all got a right to a lay.

WAY When bored with the old tried-and-true way,
As well as the dildo-in-lieu way,
    A zookeeper's wife
    Put zest in her life
By trying a "fabulous gnu way!"

WEEM A dashing young fellow named Weem
Every night had a luscious wet dream.
    'Til a friend, quite annoyed,
    Hired a disciple of Freud,
Who cured him, which I think is mean.

WEIRD

Now wouldn't most women look weird
If they grew a mustache and a beard?
   The look doesn't vex us
   If they've changed their sexes,
But women *qua* women should be sheared.

WELLS

The bishop of Bath and of Wells
Used to suffer from mysterious spells,
   And the only quick cure
   Of which he was sure
Was to fondle his monks in their cells.

WEST

There was an old critic named West
Whose penis came up to his chest.
   He said, "I declare,
   I've no pubic hair,"
So he covered his nuts with his vest.

WHALE   Jonah mused, as he cruised through the whale,
"I'm in guts to my nuts in this jail,
   But I'll pass through the ass
   In a mass of hot gas,
And depart with a fart through the tail."

WHITE   An oversexed lady named White
Insists on a dozen a night.
   A fellow named Cheddar
   Had the brashness to wed her;
His chance of survival is slight.

WHORE   An insatiable Elsinore whore
Once toured with the Met's *Trovatore*,
   But when she got through
   With a tenor she knew,
She thought she had done *Le Coq d'Or*.

WILDE   Said an unwed congressman named Wilde,
"I'm not upset at being defiled.
    My opponent's attacks
    Are no match for my tax
Plan. But now what to do with my child?"

WILDE   There was a young maiden named Wilde
Who kept herself quite undefiled
    By thinking of Jesus,
    Contagious diseases,
And the bother of having a child.

WILLOW   While Mabel lay prone 'neath a willow,
She was screwed by a large armadillo,
    And remarked to the same,
    As the two of them came,
That the next time he might bring a pillow.

WIMLEY

A wanton young woman from Wimley,
Reproached for not acting quite primly,
    Answered, "Heavens above,
    I know sex isn't love,
But it's such an attractive facsimile."

WIN

Now at college a girl just can't win,
What with studies and sex and bad gin.
    And it's just the last straw
    When the dean says, "Withdraw!"
When it's him that's been sticking it in.

WISE

A young tutor, not very wise,
Who loved to feel cocks, just for size,
    At every school dance,
    Would unzip the boys' pants;
They nicknamed him *Lord of the Flies*.

WOKINGHAM
There is a new baron of Wokingham;
The girls say he don't care for poking 'em,
Preferring "Minette,"*
Which is pleasant, but yet,
There is one disadvantage—choking 'em.

WORCESTER
There was a young lady of Worcester,
Who dreamt that a rooster sedorcester.
She awoke with a scream,
But 'twas only a dream;
A bump in the mattress had gorcester.

WYNN
Full ninety years old was friend Wynn
When he went to a hookshop to sin.
But, try as he would,
It did him no good,
For all he had left was the skin.

*Equivalent to fellatio

YEARS   While musicians have battled for years
Over which are the best symphoneers,
     They agree from the start
     That a "Whistling Fart"
Is great music to all of their rears.

YELLING   For sex our man Joe's always yelling.
At the sight of a breast's slightest swelling,
     He would pull out his cock
     From the top of his sock,
Then what he would do, there's no telling.

YORK   There was a young damsel of York
Who plugged herself up with a cork.
     She explained, "It's more svelte
     Than a chastity belt,
And is quickly removed with a fork."

YOUTH

An exuberant Westminster youth
Screwed his girl in a telephone booth.
When he pressed button "B,"
She reacted with glee,
Though onlookers deemed it uncouth.

YUMA

There was a young fellow from Yuma,
Who essayed to bugger a puma.
In the midst of the frolics,
It clawed off his bollocks;
An example of animal humor.

Reader Limericks

A Select Bibliography

There are many wonderful books of limericks that have been published over the years, a selection of which are included here. Some of them are sadly long out of print, but are worth searching out, whether at used book stores or at your local public library. Readers will also note two articles from *The Pentatette*, the Newsletter of the Limerick Special Interest Group, which also maintains a wonderful website, www.limericks.org/pentatette, featuring the modern-day stylings of many talented limericists.

Aiken, Conrad. *A Seizure of Limericks*. New York: Holt, Reinhart & Winston, 1964.

Anonymous. *To Solace the Blind*. Frankfurt-am-Main, 1945.

Baring-Gould, William S. *The Lure of the Limerick: An Uninhibited History*. New York: Clarkson N. Potter, 1967.

Backe-Hansen, William. "The Origin of the Limerick as We Know It." Moffett, CA: *The Pentatette*, Newsletter of the Limerick Special Interest Group, September 1987.

Cerf, Bennett. *Out on a Limerick*. New York: Harper & Row, 1960.

————. *Bennett Cerf's Pop-up Limericks*. New York: Random House, 1967.

Clapham, Marcus, and Rosemary Gray, eds. *A Thousand and One Limericks*. Edison, NJ: Book Sales, Inc., 2004.

Deex, Arthur. "The Assent of Limerick." Moffett, CA: *The Pentatette*, Newsletter of the Limerick Special Interest Group, October 1993.

Douglas, Norman. *Some Limericks*. Paris: Le Ballet des Muses, 1964.

Euwer, Anthony. *The Limeratomy: A Limerick Anatomy*. New York: James B. Pond, 1917.

Holland, Vyvyan. *An Explosion of Limerick*. New York: Funk & Wagnalls, 1967.

Kornberg, Harvey, illus., and Donald Hall. *The Gentleman's Alphabet Book*. New York: Penguin Putnam, 1972.

Lear, Edward. *A Book of Nonsense*. New York: Alfred A. Knopf, 1992.

Legman, Gershon. *The Limerick*. New York: Random House Value Publishing, 1991.

Perrine, Laurence. *A Limerick's Always A Verse: 200 Original Limericks*. New York: Harcourt College Publishers, 1989.

Parrott, Eric O., ed., and Robin Jacques, illus. *The Penguin Book of Limericks*. New York: Penguin, 1986.

Untermeyer, Louis, ed., and R. Taylor, illus. *Lots of Limericks*. New York: Barnes & Noble Books, 1994.

Vicarion, Count Palmira. *Book of Limericks*. Paris: The Olympia Press, 1955.

Wells, Carolyn. *Book of American Limericks*. New York: G.P. Putnam's Sons, 1925.

Limericks
Roll of Honor

In addition to those eminent scholars, cited in the bibliography, who have edited books of limericks as well as scholarly essays about the form—often enriching them with their own examples—the following composers of limericks, many of whom are represented in this volume, perhaps deserve the highest recognition and acclaim. For those composers whose names were overlooked, we offer our apologies and assure you that such oversight is purely accidental.

As for the liberties that were taken with some of the verses themselves, whether to alter the tone, the meter, or the rhymes, we beg the indulgence of the original authors and implore them to view such tinkering as a tribute to the greatness of their efforts rather than as a desecration—after all, there are countless limericks that could have been included here, but for lack of space. And for the observant readers who will no doubt see here some of the classics reconsidered, we trust that your taste for these irreverent verses has not left you insensible to the merits of occasionally updating some of them for the modern ear.

ALDISS, BRIAN W.

ANDERSON, MARY

ANDERSON, POUL

ANONYMOUS

ARMSTRONG, ROBERT PLANT

AUDEN, W.H.

BENSON, DOUG

BILLINGTON, RAYMOND A.

BISHOP, MORRIS

BOARDMAN, GEORGE

BURGESS, GELETT

CARTER, HARVEY L.

DANIELS, R. BALFOUR

DAVIES, RANDALL

DEEX, ARTHUR

DRESSLER, DAVID

FADIMAN, CLIFTON

FIELD, EUGENE

GILBERT AND SULLIVAN

GOREY, EDWARD

HERFORD, OLIVER

KIMPTON, LAWRENCE

KNOX, RONALD

LEAR, EDWARD

LEHRMAN, NAT

LINDEN, RICK

MEMBERS OF THE SOCIETY
  OF THE FIFTH LINE

MOTT, BENJAMIN

NASH, OGDEN

REED, H. LANGFORD

SEABURY, PAUL

SHAW, GEORGE BERNARD

SPECTORSKY, A.C.

STORER, NORMAN W.

TWAIN, MARK

UNTERMEYER, LOUIS

WRIGHT, GEORGE C.

Index of Fifth Lines

Note: Entries marked with ● indicate a limerick of unorthodox dimension. The fifth line is always cited, even when there are more than five lines; when there are fewer than five lines, the last line is cited.

A

"To WASHINGTON, D.C. and A.C." (Casey)

To bugger his wife in A-FLAT. (Pratt)

Of a Haydn octet in A MAJOR. (Bäger)

"It's abstinence I view with ABHORRENCE!" (florence)

Do you know a good man for ABORTIONS? (proportions)

He catches his wife in the ACT. (Bract)

Who thought her behind was ADORABLE. (deplorable)

The front of his pants would ADVANCE A LOT. (Lancelot)

His nose out of private AFFAIRS. (Benares)

Which is why she was never AFRAID. (maid)

"I'm saving that fellow for AFTER." (Shafter)

Again and again and AGAIN. (Maine)

And asked her to do it AGAIN. (Spain)

And again and again and AGAIN. (Spain) ●

"And I do it again and AGAIN." (Spain)

Kept her ever from forging AHEAD. (Stead)

On a thorn and start losing AIR. (Clair)
And his rifle went off in the AIR. (Kildare)
"Don't just lie there, vagina AKIMBO!" (limbo)
"But in Kansas they're viewed with ALARM." (farm)
And a girl in the bleachers named ALICE. (Dallas)
No phallus in Dallas fit ALICE. (Dallas)
And found that he had none at ALL! (Bengal)
But the bug didn't feel it at ALL. (Hall)
Then extended his welcome to ALL. (Paul)
And *chacun à son goût*, after ALL. (small)
Front page, sports section, and ALL. (St. Paul)
I want this *ALLEGRO CON BRIO*." (Rio)
I think I remember... ALMOST. (boast)
"They are also a snare ANDALUSIAN!" (illusion)
For people to ANIMADVERT ON. (Merton)
On a stock-market tip from ANN LANDERS. (Moll flanders)
"And aim for the neck, not the ANUS." (Janus)
'Twas the peter of Paul the APOSTLE. (Gossal)
Was a treat of enormous APPEAL. (Beal)
But the dangle, she felt, was APPEALING. (Darjeeling)
"But I *do* wish you'd take off your ARMOR." (Parma)
That he brought up his heavy ARTILLERY. (Hilary)
And remarked it was called his ASGARD. (scarred)
And lightning came out of his ASS. (Alsace) ●
"I'll have to get one with a fatter ASS." (Cape Hatteras)
"And pinches and pains in the ASS." (lass)
And bit a piece out of his ASS. (Madras)
And the band at the Waldorf ASTORIA. (Gloria)
And his penis would snap to ATTENTION. (mention)
But slept with them all in the ATTIC. (Nattick)
"And, at all times, in formal ATTIRE." (Sweet Briar)

Two eunuchs, one ape, and four **AUNTS**. (Byzance)
And now all her sisters are **AUNTS**. (France)
Or are they from one of her **AUNTS**? (transplants)
Which he'd nicknamed the "**AUTO DA FÉ**." (gay)
Which he kept in an underground **AVIARY**. (Avery)
And he wore all his foreskin **AWAY**. (Bombay)
And make the men of the world fade **AWAY**! (Faye)
Until she got carried **AWAY**. (Kay)

B

And cry, "I'm a Kushite **BABOON**!" (Asgalun)
From Johann Sebastian **BACH**. (Iraq)
"If they'd only transplanted one **BALL**!" (gall)
But nobody asked her to **BALL**. (St. Paul)
And lowered him down by his **BALLS**. (Rawls)
The bishop of London said, "**BALLS**!" (St. Paul's)
For his penis, his ass, and his **BALLS**. (St. Paul's)
I'll transplant them and make your **BALSWORTHY**! (Shaw)
"And put a pulse in the **BANANA**?" (Hannah)
So they nicknamed her Smokey the **BARE**! (Claire)
One prick, and two balls...quite a **BARGAIN**! (Morgan)
When she crashed homosexual **BARS**. (Marrs)
And carrying her tits in a **BASKET**. (A-Tasket)
Like the roar of a double **BASSOON**. (Rangoon)
Someone cried, "There's June Cleaver's **BEAVER**!" (Eva)
He creamed all over the **BEDDING**. (Reading)
"If the rest of the fleet hadn't **BEEN**." (marine)
But think of the fun it has **BEEN**!" (Racine)
Would not be held back by **BEGINNERS**. (McWhinners)
To her happy amoral **BEHAVIOR**. (Moravia)
And be jailed for indecent **BEHAVIOUR**. (Belgravia)

He died in this awful BELIEF. (Khief)
Popping off when it got two BELOW. (Citeaux)
And anything else that was BENT. (Kent)
"The tongue of my girlfriend, BERNIECE." (Greece)
She said, "I really look best in my BERSKINE." (Erskine)
And the tools of the fools who BESTRODE HER. (Baroda)
And it took a long time to get BETTER. (Gambetta)
She exclaimed, "I already feel BETTER!" (Loretta)
"And there's still fifteen inches BETWEEN US!" (Venus)
Told his date she'd be stuck with the BILL! (McGill)
And woke up the house with his BITCHIN'. (Hitchin)
And he leisurely chewed them to BITS. (Ritz)
Which kindled a wonderful BLAZE. (Hayes)
Then he BLEW IT. (France) ●
And the upshot was, young Pruitt BLEW IT. (Pruitt)
Until both of his balls had turned BLIOUX. (Sioux)
We always serve pressed duck in cold BLOOD. (dud)
When the red in his balls turned to BLUE. (screw)
And his head is all that turns BLUE. (shrew)
"When's this damn hotel get to BOISE?" (Joisey)
Then lost it right there in the BOOTH. (Duluth)
And once in a telephone BOOTH. (Duluth) ●
She gives them all straight BORDELAISE. (Glaze)
"But they always fall out of my BOX!" (Cox)
And then had it sucked by a BOY. (Troy)
Was the very same thing, but in BRAILLE. (frail)
And his penis was found in BRAZIL. (Phil)
"But that's sure FDS on your BREATH!" (Beth)
Made the bishop of Chichester's BRITCHES STIR. (Chichester)
He croaked like an old BRONTOSAURUS. (Taurus)
Which caused a slight raising of BROWS. (carouse)

And now she is sadder BUDWEISER. (Anheuser)
"But my bowels are all right. Do you BUGGER?" (lugger)
"And some bub-bub-bub-bub-bub-bub-BUTTER." (Calcutta)
"Let's open them up, bye and BYE." (high)

C

Bach's G-Minor Suite to C-SHARP. (Tharp)
"But it does make me feel like a CAD." (bad)
And he developed an unholy CALLOUS. (Hollis)
"Perhaps it's because I always try to get as many dirty words in
    the last line as I possibly CAN." (Japan) ●
And buggered himself with a CANDLE. (Handel)
"I would if I could but I CAN'T." (Grant)
And the other's the size of a CAR. (Lamar)
"But I swear, now you're there, I don't CARE." (Claire)
To which she replied, "I'll take CARE O' YA." (Bulgaria)
"I refuse to be fucked in the CARRIAGE." (Harridge)
And now he can satisfy CATTLE. (Seattle)
Save prolonged and restrained CELIBATION. (nation)
Was to fondle his monks in their CELLS. (Wells)
"But here it's a matter of CHANCE." (France)
"Had he not willed the thing to a CHARITY." (Gherrity)
Of their wives' extramarital CHEATING. (Keating)
He replied, "And in your case, some CHEEK!" (Monique)
"Tonight there'll be fucking!" (Loud CHEERS.) (Algiers)
"We must all live on alum and CHEESE!" (Florida Keys)
He found there were seeds in her CHERRY. (McNary)
And the rooster seducing the CHICKEN. (Mohican)
And the bother of having a CHILD. (Wilde)
"Plan. But now what to do with my CHILD?" (Wilde)
And my daughter's applying to CHOATE. (vote)

There is one disadvantage—**CHOKING 'EM**. (Wokingham)
And had to stay that way until **CHRISTMAS**. (Isthmus)
And then she could screw the whole **CITY**. (Nefertiti)
Involved half of the men in the **CITY**. (pretty)
"Or, shit, maybe it's only the **CLAP**...." (Fort Knapp)
Ten weeks later, he still has the **CLAP**. (Lapp)
And was perfectly simple to **CLEAN**. (Racine)
And if that is no record, it's **CLOSE**. (Montrose)
"And wink at the man in the **CLOSET**?" (Deposit)
That's the true story of Bonnie and **CLYDE**. (cried)
Her brother was named **CO-RESPONDENT**. (Sondant)
But 'twas done with the end of his **COCK**. (Kroch)
And took off for Paris, quite **COCKY**. (Saki)
To the horror of several old **CODGERS**. (Rodgers)
While he fed the bed bags of **COINS**. (Des Moines)
But how can I sleep with this **COLD BUG**? (rolled rug)
"For, you see, I'm a boxtop **COLLECTOR**." (Hector)
"They are whores of a different **COLOR**." (Muller)
The woman stayed in a deep **COMA**. (Oklahoma)
He replied, "Don't you mean see and **COME**?" (Blum)
"Then, instead of going, you'll **COME**." (glum)
And allow you to pay as you **COME**. (some)
You won't know if you're going or **COMING**. (rumming)
He suffers from a kilt **COMPLEX**. (Rex)
"With matters that do not **CONCERN YA**." (hernia)
Of the bishop while he was **COONFIRMING 'EM**. (Birmingham) ●
The tilt of his kilt caused **CONFUSION**. (MacFooshan)
"Would you radder we fuckt or **CONVOIST**?" (boist)
(The critical comment was " **COOL**.") (Poole)
She burned a red flayer in her **COONT**. (Loont)
There was fuzz on top of her **COOZIE**. (Suzie)

After all, folks, the term's **COPULATION**. (nation)
Though a lot can be done on the **COUCH**…. (grouch)
He simply got tired of **COUNTING**. (mountain)
"And the pituitary gland from *mmmmmmy* **COW**." (Dow)
And in icy conditions he **CRAWLS**. (Twin Falls)
Who ate them and thought they were **CREAMS**. (Rheims)
And she cried and she cried and she **CRIED**. (Bryde)
It was the start of organized **CRIME**. (dime)
And bigamy, sir, is a **CRIME**!" (Lyme)
And the knees of the man who had **CROSSED HER**. (Gloucester)
But his girl thought his root was still **CUTE**. (boot)

D

And that was the end of her **DATES**. (Bates)
And practically useless on **DATES**. (Gates)
Just ask any one of my **DAUGHTERS**. (waters)
And beating his meat below **DECK**. (Peck)
That's when knighthood was truly **DEFLOWERED**! (coward)
"Or else it's the Lux I've **DEFLOWERED**." (Howard)
A sheep in Hyde Park. 'Twas **DELIGHTFUL**. (frightful)
And was cast into the Lions' **DEN**. (men)
And remark, "This one'll really **DESTROLLA**!" (La Jolla)
When I know it took place in **DETROIT**. (adroit)
"I have just read a book—**DEUTERONOMY**!" (bonhomie)
But made a wonderful gambling **DEVICE**. (Brice)
In the fit of a friend's **DIAPHRAGM**. (East Birmingham)
She was grateful for getting first **DIBS**. (Cribbs) ●
He suffered, whatever he **DID**. (Madrid)
Who said that he would…and he **DID**. (Madrid)
But he had a good time of it, **DIDN'T HE**? (Sidney)
He could not have been wronger: it **DIDNA**. (McSidney)

But in the end he used a big **DILDA**. (Hilda)

And knew she had met with **DISASTER**. (Astor)

Thus causing domestic **DISSENSION**. (abstention)

"I'm too ancient to find this **DISTRESSIN'**." (McKesson)

Whose wife's tastes ran to the **DIURNAL**. (colonel)

"If you know what I mean…and I'm pretty damn sure that you **DO**." (Kew) ●

But the bull figured out what to **DO**. (Soo)

But his girl kept insisting, "Well **DONE!**" (fun)

"Them birds is reserved for the **DONS!**" (St. John's)

He preferred *A Midsummer Night's* **DREAM**. (seem)

And munch it without even **DRESSING**. (Lessing)

While at night, it's in close-ardor **DRILLING**. (Trilling)

Which is why Tripp has postnaval **DRIP**. (Tripp)

And afterwards serve as a **DUSTER**. (Buster)

E

She was finally bedded with **E'S**. (Pease)

Caressing a penis with **EARS**. (Sears)

"I really must watch what I **EAT**." (Pete)

"I'm a slow but fastidious **EATER**." (Lolita)

Till he unwound it, eenwich by **EENWICH**. (Greenwich)

For my mourning becomes **ELECTRA**. (spectra)

"But you still might have fun in the **EMBERS**." (members)

And the head of a kid just **EMERGIN'**. (Spitzbergen)

He could bugger six Greeks **EN BROCHETTE**. (Tibet)

"Hush, love, thou'st spoiled Paradise **ENOW**." (Bough)

"For clerical rates, please **ENQUIRE**." (Maguire)

Was never again so **ENTICING**. (Tyson)

"But only for high-rise **ERECTIONS**." (imperfections)

And left by the fire **ESCAPE**. (rape)

Merrill Lynch, Goldman Sachs, ET CETERA. (hetera)
And, in turn, poxed all the cocks in EUTOXETER. (Eutoxeter)
His putting his dick to good EWES. (Crews)
On the end of the dong, graft an EYE. (try)

F

"This is art with a capital F!" (McNeff)
Then returned with a smile on his FACE. (grace)
And for his sins wound up losing FACE. (Grace)
But it's such an attractive FACSIMILE." (Wimley)
But the scent—well, that was a FAILIA. (Australia)
Her husbands have all turned out to be FAIRIES. (Aries)
And slave girls who danced with a FAN. (Poitan)
"What a blessing," he said, "I'm not FASTER." (Astor)
Which proves that the turtle was FERTILE. (Myrtle)
"For revenge I'll give her athlete's FETUS!" (Cletus)
"The customer always comes FIRST." (Hearst)
And in concert he jerked off with his FIST. (Liszt)
And twenty-two yards of red FLANNEL! (Kannel)
For her costume did not keep her FLESH IN. (Gression)
And now she's in bed with the FLU! (Peru)
"Should all come equipped with a FLY." (cry)
"I shall stick to my old Spanish FLY." (Frei)
And brandish it about like a FOIL. (Doyle)
Appeared in the summer school FOLDER. (Boulder)
It was useless for what it was FOR. (Cawnpore)
And practice the art of FORBEARANCE. (Clarence)
But it's something he'd rather FORGET. (Set)
"And is quickly removed with a FORK." (York)
They think of us Earthlings as FRAIL. (male)
"If permitted to coign a FRAISE." (Mays)

Through using the letters of FRANCE. (Penzance)
So all he could shoot was FRAPPÉ. (Norway)
And only revived when lanced FREELY. (Greely)
That informs all arrivals: FUCK QUEUE. (few)
And quietly murmured, "FUCK THEE!" (Lee)
I'll translate: It says FUCK YOU ALL. (wall)
"On the grounds of inadequate FUN." (Munn)
Made him skip it as being too FUNNY. (money)

G

Without even leaving the G'RAGE. (Lodge)
He gave her a valeigh, by GALEIGH! (Raleigh)
A moose and a goose and a 'GATOR. (Ada)
Just above his huge male GENITALIA. (Thalia)
Just how alien can you GET? (pet)
So everyone plied her with GIN. (Flynn)
Through a crack in her chastity GIRDLE. (Myrtle)
"Spread your legs, dear, you're breaking my GLASSES!" (masses)
And she emerged transfigured with GLEE. (Capri)
Wasn't Tom, Dick, or Harry—but GLENDA! (Brenda)
Three balls and a purple GOATEE. (Dundee)
A bump in the mattress had GORCESTER. (Worcester)
Who said it was worth what he GOT…. (Shalott) ●
But the boy from the smithy GOT IN. (East Lynne)
It was gray, had long ears, and ate GRASS. (Madras)
"Don't wait 'til your hair has turned GRAY." (lay)
But otherwise doing just GREAT. (Kate)
"Though I'd say your physique is just GREAT." (state)
Was "God Bless Our Home," done in GREEN. (Levine)
Through Doppler effect, showed as GREEN. (limousine)
And brought her a leaf from the GREEN-H'US. (Aenos)

My God! How his business has GROWN! (Bone)
Which solved all his problems, I GUESS! (Loch Ness)
Guillotine! Guillotine! GUILLOTINE! (obscene)

H

And had a lascivious HABIT. (Babbit)
So he mounted the ladder and HAD HER. (madder)
There were only two balls, and he HAD 'EM. (Adam)
"And I come when I'm combing my HAIR." (McNair)
"How 'bout thirty-four and a HALF?" (laugh)
And was had by the dog in the HALL. (Bengal)
Are the sick, and the lame, and the HALT." (Walt)
Though in secret Noah sometimes ate HAM. (jam)
"And awake with solution in HAND." (land)
And the organ of George Frederick HANDEL. (Crandall) ●
Or mine, and not one half so HARD. (Bard)
Could help them to get pretty HARD. (Barnard)
"When the telephone rings, I can't HEAR." (fear)
And started up HEARSE RENT-A-CAR. (Barr)
Of such is the kingdom of HEAVEN... (Devon)
And the prize horse's ass in all HISTORY. (mystery)
"Sir, you are playing the wrong HOLE." (droll)
"I'm so glad it wasn't a HORNET." (St. Bees) ●
Discovering, too late, 'twas for HORSES. (Tarsus)
Because, she said, she was HOT IN 'EM. (Tottenham)
An example of animal HUMOR. (Yuma)
"Who was known as Attila the HUNG!" (clung)
Including, alas, her own HYMEN. (men)
She died happy of HYPERMAMMALIA. (Dahlia)

I

"Thank goodness you're stronger than I AM!" (Siam)

"You may call me a bugger. I AM!" (Siam)

Is democracy better? I ESK YOU. (Lupescu)

And murmur, "*Ich liebe, ICH LIEBE.*" (Sheba)

"As long as it's total IMMERSION." (conversion)

See, he lacked diplomatic IMMUNITY. (community)

But the head on his wand most IMPRESSED HER. (Chester)

When it's him that's been sticking it IN. (win)

"'Til my husband became INDIFFERENT!" (Brent)

Cried the maiden, "The buck is INFLATED!" (elated)

At a quarter past ten it was IN HER (Skinner) ●

To add incest to insult and INJURY. (gingery)

But what he heard was, "Come on INSIDE!" (Clyde)

But he read an old *Playboy* INSTEAD. (Bay Head)

"Won't you swallow my pride, dear, INSTEAD?" (Ted)

Curable only with shots INTRA-VENUS. (Salinas)

Lest a curious eye should INTRUDE. (Jude)

She kept asking, "Hey, Pop! IS IT IN?" (Berlin)

I wonder what happened to IT? (tit)

Rose said, "Yes, and, by Jesus, they're ITCHIN'!" (McMitchin)

J

It's the fellow in front gets the JAR. (star)

That burn in their skirts and their JEANS. (teens) ●

That she mashed all her partners to JELLY. (Corelli)

Instead of petroleum JELLY. (Kelly)

Just in time to give it a JERK. (McGurk)

Though it involves frequent trips to the JOHN. (Huan)

"Well, if we can't lick 'em, let's JOIN 'EM." (Bynum)

"Than sleep with that bitch JOSEPHINE." (serene)

K

That shows where you see Eph you see **KAY**. (Kay)
And screwed his poor wife with the **KEY**. (Dundee)
"For which I won't give him the **KEY**?" (McGee)
"What I need is that greasy **KID STUFF**." (King's Bluff)

L

And blew kisses at the profs with her **LABIA**. (Arabia)
And complaints from the women he **LAID**. (Port Said)
An organ admittedly **LARGE**. (Marge)
"Since your screws have been rusty of **LATE**." (mate)
And smelled like a broken **LATRINE**. (dream)
But we've all got a right to a **LAY**. (way)
She thought she had done *LE COQ D'OR*. (whore)
"Mon Dieu! Aprés moi, LE DELUGÉ." (Bruges)
"It's a game where I'm blowing the **LEAD**!" (Freed)
"I know, for I've had him in **LEICESTER**." (Chester)
Or, as Mexicans say, 'Peon **LEON**!'" (Leon)
"Please list your sins in your **LETTER**." (Gambetta)
You expected this line to be **LEWD**. (strewed)
"Just the same as she'd acted in **LIFE**!" (fife)
Who supplied him a new lease on **LIFE**! (Fyfe)
She died with a smile on her **LIPS**. (Phipps)
Now she's known as **LITTLE MISS MUFFIT**. (Tuphet)
Now he's worn by his girl in a **LOCKET**. (Milnocket)
He transplanted it up to the **LOFT**. (Croft) ●
To pull him around **LONDONDERRY**. (Glengarry)
She replied, "Like a man, only **LONGER**." (Batonger)
They nicknamed him *LORD OF THE FLIES*. (wise)
But his balls hung out—and he **LOST 'EM**. (Boston)
"Of an anteater's tongue tops the **LOT**." (Malotte)

M

She could play "To a Wild Rose" by MACDOWELL. (Rowell)
From New York to the Straits of MAGELLAN. (Dunellen)
With twelve kids in old MANDALAY. (Bombay)
Plus hair from a dog with the MANGE. (strange)
A source of amusement to MANY. (Kilkenny)
"And the other we'll do after MARRIAGE." (Harwich)
But could never quite manage a MARROW. (Harrow)
And, he *thinks,* the left knocker of MARS. (Lars)
And be doctored before she is MASTERED. (plastered)
Mutual MASTURBATORIUM. (emporium)
Who had a square root to MATCH. (Hatch)
Whether splitting's as much fun as MATING. (stating)
"Now one of them's running for MAYOR." (Hare)
Named Lincoln Dean "Douglas" MCARTHA. (Martha)
"You poked the wrong organ in ME!" (he)
And felt it was one-up to ME. (Lee)
Said the plumber, still plumbing, "It's ME!" (Leigh)
"Of the captain, the boatswain, and ME." (sea)
And everyone thought it was ME! (tea)
Who cured him, which I think is MEAN. (Weem)
Was made of his MEMBRUM VIRILE. (Reilly)
Must be viewed in projection MERCATOR! (Crater)
To just a bit short of a METER. (neater)
And polished her off in MID-AIR. (Adair)
Then she gave him a piece of her MIND. (dined)
"What a night for a blow! Come, MON—SOON!" (Rangoon)
"That comes of not frigging since MONDAY!" (Lundy)
And a beard on a nude by MONET. (de Bray)
"But I can always come back for MORE." (Gore)
"I think I've discovered one MORE WAY." (Norway)

"At the wheel of my two-seater **MORRIS**." (Norris)
"Give your sons to the church," was his **MOTTO**. (Giotto)
"Than ever went in by your **MOUTH**!" (Louth)
"Then denies me the use of her **MUFF**!" (McGuff)
For the bustle turned out to be **MUSCLE**. (Russell)
Being charged with corrupting a **MYNAH**. (China)

N

"But extruded from fatherly **NATES**." (Mithridates)
Or released for his amorous **NEEDS**. (Leeds)
On his flame-throwing fiddle./Signed, **NERO**. (hero) ●
And he found himself totally **NEUTER**. (tutor)
And was lavishly praised by the *NEWS*. (Cruz)
He should not have worn frilly lace **NIGHTIES**. (Stylites)
Her need for resistance was **NIL**. (McSwill)
"It is driving us *NON COMPOST MENTIS*." (*in loco parentis*)
"God knows, it is better than **NONE**." (Verdun)
And then he would come through the **NOSE**. (Mose) ●
She lodges in Pimlico **NOW**. (Slough)
She said to her questioner, "**NUTS**!" (Stutz)
But what could he do with it? **NUTTIN'**. (Dutton)

O

He prefers to be tying one **OFF**! (Goff)
Lynne said, "No, but I visit there **OFTEN**." (McCoffin)
When the prick should have been in **OPHELIA**. (congeal ya)
Or similar duties employed **ON**. (Croydon)
"They call what they do **OUTERCOURSE**." (course)
At which point they were both **OVERCOME**. (Crumm)
"A mighty poor thing, but mine **OWN**!" (Stone)
There's no thrill in sex for the **OYSTER**. (cloister)
And Bavarian cream on the **OYSTERS**. (boisterous)

P

And her asshole in Buckingham **PALACE**. (Alice)

And kept her from playing the **PALACE**. (Alice)

But was grand when he got in her **PANTS**. (France)

Was replaced by a motorized **PANZER**. (Cancer)

"Ya do it much faster than **PAR**." (Carr)

And fondling nude statues in **PARKS**. (marks)

And was glad to be doing her **PART**. (Lionheart)

She had asked a more pertinent **PART**. (tart)

And figured out that she'd rather **PASS**. (class)

"I'm embarrassed when peanuts are **PASSED**." (last)

And Tolstoi the one seeking **PEACE**. (niece)

And it even takes two just to **PEE**. (three)

And now the poor cowboy can't **PEE-O**. (Leo)

But his rhythm: iambic **PENTAMETER**. (McNamiter)

"I come in my pants. It's **PERNICIOUS**!" (vicious)

"Or is it a trick of **PERSPECTIVE**?" (detective)

And at night they get up to **PERVERSIONS**. (Persians)

"I *prefer* polymorphous **PERVERSITY**." (University)

I'll stick to my old rubber **PESS'RY**!" (ne's'ry)

The right church, so to speak, but wrong **PEW**. (Purdue)

"But, you see, I am high on **PEYOTE**!" (Don Quixote) ●

They cling to their old-fashioned **PHALLUSES**. (picture palaces)

They found a real cod in his **PIECE**. (Nice)

That the next time he might bring a **PILLOW**. (willow)

Then go to the garden and **PISS**. (miss)

Was found without substance or **PITH**. (Smith)

"But I still want to keep my **PLAYPEN**." (sin)

For an orgy's a horny of **PLENTY**!" (Henty)

By insisting, "first hocus—then **POKE US**!" (Hohokus)

And she prefers richer to **POORER**! (Cora)

But one dubbed it pure POPPYCOCK. (Jacques)
And *Italy* back round her PORKS. (South Forks)
And I do not collect PORNOGRAPHICKER. (trafficker)
But got stuck in the fifteenth POSITION. (mission)
"I can beat any jerk, pound for POUND!" (crowned)
"To un *homme virile*, poussy is POUSSY!" (Sans Souci)
And his organ got raves in the PRESS. (Kress)
(Under the sheets, we PRESUME). (doom)
But the other won numerous PRIZES. (Devizes)
His favorite hue remains PUCE. (Roos)
His career had been nipped in the PUD. (flood)
And reviled them while pulling his PUD. (Robin Hood)
"But I got a good price for the PUPS." (Tupps)
For the pleasure of hearing it PURR. (Ur)
"There wasn't much room to PUT MUCH IN." (Metuchen)

Q

To McHugh spelling *fuq* (with a Q). (McHugh)
At present, Miss Hoople's QUADRUPLE. (Hoople)
She's been voted the Humcoming QUEEN. (Doreen) ●
"Save the Weasel' from 'Pop Goes the QUEEN.'" (Marine)
And burnt all the hair off her QUIM. (Tring)
Instead of his mom's ample QUIMMER. (dimmer)
Or make it as big as a QUOIT. (Detroit) ●

R

It seems consistency gave him a RASH. (Dash)
"Have a new prostate gland, I'd much RATHER." (Mather)
"This is one thing those bastards can't RATION!" (fashion)
And pretzels came out of the REAR. (Lear)
Is great music to all of their REARS. (years)

I am sure it's a rare RECREATION. (nation)
And all of her nights in REHEARSING. (McPherson)
Which, these days, is far more RELIABLE? (viable)
"And strollers don't make snide REMARKS." (larks)
And was famed for her bright REPARTEE. (Tralee)
"They can play with themselves," she REPLIED. (Hyde)
"It's simply a case of RETOOLING." (Souling)
She demanded nocturnal REVANCHE. (Blanche)
She replied, "You're not in the RIGHT ONE." (Brighton)
And he came without even a RIPPLE. (Tipple)
"You're supposed to be Peter—a ROCK!" (flock)
Was nicknamed "the piece of the ROCK." (Locke)
She backed in as a Pillsbury ROLL. (Kroll)
And christened them Myrtle and ROSE. (Montrose)
Still, a rose is a rose is a ROSE. (unclose)
"Will that prevent the onset of ROT?" (Dot)
In the Andrew J. Mellon ROTUNDA. (Burunda)
Once he jumped thirteen girls in a ROW! (Lowe)
She had one rubber bub and one RUBBABLE. (Hasdrubbable)
And a water pump covered in RUST. (St. Just)

S

Conjugating all day in the SACK. (hack)
Without even wetting the SAILS. (Wales)
"The stew is too flat and needs SALTING." (halting)
And lost both his stones for the SAME. (Notre Dame)
Said, "My name is Simpson…not SAMSON." (Ransom)
"And I'll take your name off the list, SCHNOOK." (look)
"Of the great Archimedean SCREW." (Peru)
For the fellows would peek but not SCREW! (Pru)
"But, frankly, I'd much rather SCREW." (Purdue)

"And I pass up too damn many SCREWS." (Hughes)
In rubbers they float to the SEA. (lea)
But the gal was allergic to SEAMEN. (Leeman)
"Side's good for more than finding a SEAT ON." (Eton)
And sideways she couldn't be SEEN. (Green)
Why, then he'd start making the SEEN. (McQueen)
While his anus blew SEMPER FIDELIS. (Ellis)
In order to pee by SEPTEMBER. (member)
"Here're two tablets; they're called SERUTAN." (man)
While the Chorus sang songs about SEX. (Oedipus Rex)
The distinguishing mark of his SEX AT HER. (Exeter)
"And something is wrong with the SHAPE." (Cape)
To wear my poor cat as a SHAWL. (ball)
And had to go home in a SHAWL. (St. Paul)
So did SHE. (Dee) ●
But women *qua* women should be SHEARED. (weird)
"Not to win or to place, but to SHOW!" (slow)
Where you wouldn't believe, if not SHOWN. (Joan)
Saying gently, "Etaoin SHRDLU." (askew)
"You've a virginal clam? I could SHUCK IT." (Nantucket) ●
And now they're interred, side by SIDE. (McBride)
"Well, *this* won't be much of a SIN." (Lynn)
He remarked, "If I play, will you SING?" (king)
It's engaged in 1000110100100 or 69? (fine)
For all he had left was the SKIN. (Wynn)
His chance of survival is SLIGHT. (White)
The other, remarkably, SMALLER. (Mahler)
To display the most quimsical SMILE. (Kyle)
"The son-of-a-bitch only SMILED!" (McWilde)
"Sit down, and I'll play you a SNATCH." (Hatch)
And pissed in his whisky and SODA. (Swoboda)

And besides which, they never went SOFT. (Croft)

"But I'm sorry you came quite so SOON." (Thun)

As an oversized lyric SOPRANO. (Havana)

"Let's lift up the top-sheet and SPANKER." (Bangor)

"Make it flutter about like a SPARROW." (Harrow)

And showed that young girl how to SPEND! (Ostend)

"For I'm damned if I'll draw 'til I SPEND!" (Ostend)

"And in short is a damned heavy SPENDER." (gender)

Were so good you could hear when you SPENT. (Brent)

And he spilled his SPERMATOZOA. (Samoa)

"For the plural of spouse is 'SPICE!'" (Dice)

And smirked to her spouse, "Let us SPRAY!" (Bray)

"With an ass that's like Jell-O on SPRINGS." (King's)

That left several permanent STAINS. (Raines)

It forced her to screw STANDING UP. (renown) ●

Was the only thing he could keep STIFF. (Schiff)

So thick it was like a mink STOLE. (soul)

"I'd call this the tenth-inning STRETCH." (kvetch)

She found herself at Sunset, STRIPPED. (hipped)

He changed hands without missing a STROKE. (Oak)

"While you lay in inebriate STUPOR." (Cooper)

She was tight-lipped about her SUCCESS! (Bess)

Launched him into the mouth of one SUE. (Lou)

"That would ruin my Nutcracker SUITE." (Crete)

Made him feel SUPERCALIFRAGILISTICEXPIALIDOCIOUS. (Moses) ●

And made her a Mother SUPERIOR. (Siberia)

She replied, "That's a hard one to SWALLOW!" (Rollo)

"It's so very much easier to SWALLOW!" (sallow)

"And my ankles occasionally SWELL." (Nell)

And that lift that he'd asked for was SWIFT! (drift)

T

As he lovingly busses each TABLE. (Gable)

"And depart with a fart through the TAIL." (whale)

Leads to pregnancy, isn't life TAME? (name)

With a musical sigh like a TANGO. (Durango)

He died of old age at the TASK. (Trask)

She found there was no tit for TAT. (begat)

Then what he would do, there's no TELLING. (yelling)

He had to search for a perch with a TERRIER. (Bulgaria)

"I will help you bone up for the TEST." (Miss West)

Two earrings carved from his TESTICLES. (popsicles)

Were engaged in bizarre TÊTE-À-TÊTE. (fête)

So he wrote her a letter to THANK HER. (anchor)

On seventeenth-century THEMES. (Rheims)

"I'd have to consult a THESAURUS." (Doris)

"If you'd pay some attention to THESE." (St. Bees)

To lengthen and strengthen and THICKEN 'EM. (Twickenham)

So she can goose herself in the THIGHSES. (Pisces)

"To provide an additional THRILL." (McGill)

"And I quoted you ten bucks a THROE." (flo)

I will never admit I am THROUGH. (Although)

"As soon as the service is THROUGH." (knew)

Cries of "Shame!" "Kick his ass!" " THROW HIM OUT!" (mahout)

"But what has become of my THUMB?" (Crumm)

Or the end of her calloused old THUMB. (McComb)

"Never mind," somebody said, "you're probably dehydrated;
    just give it TIME." (Versailles) ●

And keep her abreast of the TIMES. (Grimes)

Now he's called by his friends TINKERBELL. (Big Dell)

At the end, she said, "Thanks for the TIP." (Kip)

Made him tireder and tireder and TIREDER. (Bryerder)

That *The Lady in Red* was by **TITIAN**. (Mission)
And conjugate with her boyfriend **TOBIAS**. (Elias)
Now he's nursing clap of the **TOE**. (Bordeaux)
Six aldermen were kissing his **TOKUS**. (Hohokus)
It utterly ruined his **TONE**. (Cohn)
"Do you have any seats for **TONIGHT**?" (site)
"Or the rest will be wanting one, **TOO**." (Crewe)
"To tutor two tutors to **TOOT**?" (flute)
But was fatally crushed on a **TOOTH**. (forsooth)
Are the high-heel holes thrust through the **TOP**. (stop)
That the end of the rubber was **TORN**. (Cape Horn)
"So I'd welcome some feminine **TORQUE**." (New York)
"With the wrestling coach and the **TRAINER**." (plainer)
"Is a thought that's forever **TRANCE-PLANTED**?" (ranted)
That his wife was an ord'nary **TROLLOP**. (Polyp)
And so began the "old college **TRY**." (Frye)
And she didn't know which way to **TURN**. (Laverne)
And she'd wink at the prof with her **TWIDGET**. (Bridget)
I'dve called it *One Tail and* **TWO TITTIES**. (Two Cities)
Of this bisexual built just for **TWO**! (Kew)

U

Thus shocking the **ULTRA-FASTIDIOUS**. (Phidias)
"For a Frenchman, one egg is *UN OEUF*!" (Maloff)
Though onlookers deemed it **UNCOUTH**. (youth)
All while wearing her **UNDERPANTSY**. (Nanci)
And he said, "Vy, it's zimple; look **UNDRUM**." (Vundrum)
"But a llama! There's numero **UNO**!" (Bruno)
Got a grip and refused to **UNPUCKER**. (Tucker)
Until *after* she found he'd **UPKNOCKTOR**. (Proctor)
And shattered the bedroom **UTENSIL**. (Stensall)

V

She muttered, "How Green Was My **VALET**!" (Sally)
Crapped chocolate, orange ice, and **VANILLA**. (Manila)
In postures ingenious and **VARIOUS**. (Sagittarius)
"Pardon me while I pee in this **VASE**." (Chase)
"To pound a man into my **VENT**." (Kent)
Left him dead upon the **VERANDA**. (Parmimahanda)
So he covered his nuts with his **VEST**. (West)
While exulting, "My pleasure's **VICARIOUS**!" (nefarious)
He would let the fart bitch…and **VICE VERSA**! (bursar)

W

"My initials are **W.C.**" (Dundee)
By filigree chains from her **WAIST**. (taste)
"What offspring we'll leave in our **WAKE**!" (Lake)
Someone there is who doesn't love a **WALL**. (crawl)
So her little base-burner could **WARM YA**. (Formia)
"That isn't a prick—it's a **WART**!" (Connaught)
"I like it to last and be **WARTY**." (Del Norte)
But isn't as much fun in that **WAY**. (Green Bay)
Said a snow blower's heading this **WAY**!" (Hooray)
It's clear she has come a long **WAY**. (May)
By trying a "fabulous gnu **WAY**!" (way)
And couldn't sit down for the **WEEDS**. (Leeds)
And instead of coming, he **WENT**! (Ghent)
She knew—*Oh, she knew!*—But she **WENT**. (Kent)
She was eager to come when Lent **WENT**. (Trent)
With a flip of her feathers, "Just say **WHEN**!" (Ben)
In either how much or with **WHO**. (screw)
But it brought smiles to the lips of his **WHOA**. (Genoa)

To do what, and with which, and to WHOM. (Khartoum)
"But I can't recall exactly of WHOM." (Khartoum)
And declared it was cheaper than WHORING. (Goring)
Old Joseph tried Potiphar's WIFE. (life)
And write, draw, or color at WILL. (Bill)
And wound up in a bed of sweet WILLIAM. (Liliom)
But, at present, the other side's WINNING. (beginning)
To hear the braves holler, "WIOUX, WIOUX!" (Sioux)
"Whom it's fun to be virtuous WITH." (Smith)
"I really must build them more WOBILE." (Cantabile)

Y

"What the fuck will you do with your YANG?" (hang)
Makes it hard to get hard in the YARD. (discard)
"Gang-bang I've had in nine YEARS!" (Beers)
And run away, screamin' and YELLIN'. (Helen)
From Yok-Yok-Yok-YOKNAPATAWPHA. (offer)
"And besides, he comes quicker than YOU." (Kew)
"The Messiah will come before YOU." (Peru)
"Coming Soon in a Theater Near YOU!" (Sue)
If you think that's a cinch, see if YOU CAN. (toucan)

Z

And his real batting average was ZERO. (Nero)
And sent the results to the ZOO. (Peru)